# Praises for
## *Shut Up & Write!*

D0520099

*Shut Up & Write!* is both instructive and encouraging. Judy Bridges doesn't grand-stand, she doesn't intimidate. She's a teacher in the truest sense of the word.
— Kurt Chandler, Senior Editor, *Milwaukee Magazine*

The reason I hit the 75,000 mark in self-published book sales—Judy Bridges! She is brilliant. I am so glad that through *Shut Up & Write!* writers everywhere can now have a piece of Judy reflected in their work.
— Stacey Kannenberg, author of *Let's Get Ready for Kindergarten* and *Let's Get Ready for First Grade*

For years Judy Bridges has been helping writers perfect their craft. *Shut Up & Write!* shares her knowledge with those who do not have the privilege of work-ing with her directly. I highly recommend it!
— Elaine Bergstrom, author of *Shattered Glass* and *Mina: The Dracula Story Continues*

I am a published author today, thanks to Judy Bridges. Her knowledge of writ-ing, along with her wisdom, guidance, and uncanny ability to know exactly when I needed a good kick in the pants, were essential to helping me achieve my goal of writing a book. I couldn't have done it without her.
— Jill Morin, author of *Better Make It Real*

For many years I wanted to write a novel about World War Two. Judy Bridges' patience and "pull no punches" style of critique transformed my writing into a craft that caught the eye of a publisher, and my dream was fulfilled.
— Douglas W. Jacobson, author of *Night of Flames*

*Shut Up & Write!* is the cumulative wisdom of the best writing teacher around. Judy Bridges has made a difference in the lives and careers of thousands of writers (myself included). Her wisdom comes from the best place: real experience coupled with a huge heart.
— Shannon Jackson Arnold, author of *Everybody Loves Ice Cream*

Judy Bridges is one of the most generous writing spirits I have ever met. She understands the awesome potential of a blank sheet of paper, the power of the pen, and the calling of the writer to fill the page. What a gift that she now shares her wisdom in *Shut Up & Write!*
— Sheila Hanrahan, winner of *Wisconsin Academy Review* Award for Short Fiction

Judy's voice, her irreverent sense of humor, and her acute instinct for what works and what doesn't shine through these pages. Not everyone can attend Judy's classes, but now, by reading *Shut Up & Write!*, writers at any level can tap into her many years of experience. Writing will never be quite so lonely again.
— Felicity Librie, writer of essays, articles, and fiction

If there's anyone who can help get you to say "I'm a writer" with confidence and pride, it's Judy Bridges. Whenever I see my byline in print, I say a quiet thank you to Judy for giving me the skills and encouragement I needed.
— Christi Clancy, winner of Council for Wisconsin Writers' Sternig Award for Short Fiction

Before I met Judy Bridges, I never felt like a writer. She gave me the gift of confidence. Judy's inspiration is with me as I pound out revisions for the tenth edition of my college textbook. I'm forever grateful.
— Jean Harlan, author of *Science Experiences for the Early Childhood Years* and *Science as It Happens*

Part inspiration and part how-to, *Shut Up & Write!* demystifies the writing process. Judy's genuine joy at helping others make their writing dreams come true shines through every anecdote and every bit of no-nonsense advice.
— Kim Suhr, Director, RedBird-RedOak Writing

Judy Bridges' methods have guided my writing since elementary school and are now getting me through my master's program. She's a goddess!
— Katie Lance, graduate student, American University, Washington, DC

Thank goodness Judy has finally put her thoughts and wisdom on paper!
— Paul Salsini, author of *The Cielo, Sparrow's Revenge,* and *Dino's Story*

Judy has an uncanny knack for making sure the writer, amateur or pro, knows how to move forward. Thanks to *Shut Up & Write!* and her strong encouragement, my first book will be published next year.
— Josephe Marie Flynn, SSND, author of *Rescuing Regina: The Battle to Save a Friend from Deportation and Death*

*Shut Up & Write!*—Judy's wit and wisdom condensed into one volume—is a gift to writers at any level. This book is a kick in the butt, an encouraging friend, and an experienced teacher all rolled into one.
— Karen McQuestion, author of *A Scattered Life*

# SHUT UP & write!

## JUDY BRIDGES

**REDBIRD STUDIO PRESS**
Milwaukee, Wisconsin

*Shut Up & Write!* by Judy Bridges
© 2011 by Judith Weyenberg Bridges

All rights reserved

No part of this book may be reproduced or transmitted in any form or by any means without written permission from the author, except for the inclusion of brief passages in a review.

Excerpt from *Nocturne* by Elaine Bergstrom (page 58) is reprinted with permission of the author.
Excerpt from *The Art & Science of Tracking Man and Beast* by Tom Hanratty (page 59–60) is reprinted with permission of the author.
Excerpt from "A Vision of Daffodils" by Al Martinez (page 65), which originally appeared in *Modern Maturity*, January-February 1997, is reprinted with permission of the author.
"Shades of Gray" by Robert Vaughan (page 66–67), which first appeared on www.Amphibi.us in June 2010, is reprinted with permission of the publisher.
Excerpt from "Anything that Sticks" by Sheila Hanrahan (page 74), which first appeared in *Wisconsin People & Ideas*, Vol. 56, No. 3, is reprinted with permission of the publisher.
Excerpt from *The Tiger Claw* by Shauna Singh Baldwin (page 80) is reprinted with permission of the publisher, Alfred A. Knopf, Canada.
Excerpt from "The Joker" by Kurt Chandler (page 80–81), which originally appeared in *Milwaukee Magazine*, December 2008, is reprinted with permission of the author.
Excerpt from *Hiking Michigan's Upper Peninsula* by Eric Hansen (page 81) is reprinted with permission of the publisher, Falcon Guide.

Editor: Carolyn Kott Washburne
Design and Typography: Kate Hawley
Index: Carol Roberts
Production Coordination: Susan Pittelman

First Printing 2011
Printed in the United States of America

15  14  13  12  11      1  2  3  4  5

This book is printed on acid-free paper.

ISBN-13: 978-0-9764742-7-2
Library of Congress Control Number: 2010912802


    Publisher's Cataloging-in-Publication
    (Provided by Quality Books, Inc.)

Bridges, Judy.
    Shut up & write! / Judy Bridges.
    p. cm.
    Includes bibliographical references and index.
    LCCN 2010912802
    ISBN-13: 978-0-9764742-7-2
    ISBN-10: 0-9764742-7-1

    1. Authorship.   I. Title. II. Title: Shut up and write!

PN153.B75 2011            808'.02
                QBI10-600163


Published by:
Redbird Studio Press
PO Box 70234
Milwaukee, WI 53207
www.redbirdstudio.com

This book is dedicated to:
My students, who convinced me I could teach.
My family and friends, who said I could write.
My husband, who waited.

# CONTENTS

# FIGURES

# PREFACE

I had a dream that I was at a book signing for *Shut Up & Write!* You were glowing behind a counter table, in a church kitchen (don't ask me why), and there was a long line of happy people getting their copies. We each took a numbered slip of paper, which we put our names on, and some of us who knew you were adding thank you notes for your inspiration and motivation, and then we'd turn in those slips and get our books. And that's all I remember, except I woke up feeling happy for you!

—Pam Parker, novelist and short story writer, graduate of
the Shut Up & Write! workshop at Redbird Studio

I NEVER AIMED TO BE A TEACHER, probably because I was such a lousy student that I couldn't imagine myself standing in front of a class acting as if I knew anything. All through elementary and high school, I sat in the back row with the Wagners and Wentzels and wrote notes to my friends. When Sister Beatrix, the principal of the first of three high schools I attended, called my dad into her office to discuss my behavior, I did what any sensible teenager would do: I denied it. Sister Beatrix picked up a shoebox, walked over to me, and dumped a couple hundred folded paper triangles over my head. The only thing I remember between that moment and the time I was grounded for the remainder of freshman year was hearing her say, "She's obviously going to be a writer."

To the surprise of no one who knew me then, I took a circuitous route through a few dozen jobs before I entered college, aced all my classes, finally got a bachelor's degree, and then a master's at the age of fifty-three. For many of those years, I earned my living as a writer, until one day a friend said, "Why don't you teach a workshop?" I thought that was a dumb idea, did it anyway, and that was the beginning of Redbird Studio, a writing center located on the top floor of an old convent boarding school in Milwaukee.

The studio name was a figment of my imagination. I "saw" a bird that looked like a swallow except that it was red, ascending, really striving, flying high. My husband sketched the bird on a sticky note and that became the logo for the big, windowed room in which I led three to five workshops a week, including a class called Shut Up & Write!

More than six thousand students later, I can say I've found my bliss. I love writing and the whole concept of communication, but the thing that thrills me most is seeing the look on another writer's face when the words finally come out right. When that happens to one of my students—and it happens often—I take full credit for it, whether I deserve it or not. I smile when I think about writers like:

**Kirk Farber,** the red-headed musician whose debut novel, *Postcards From a Dead Girl,* was one of four Redbird novels that made it to the semifinals in the first Amazon-Penguin Breakthrough Novel Awards, and was published by Harper Perennial.

**Christi Clancy,** whose short stories appeared in *Glimmer Train* and *Hobart Journal* and who won a Council for Wisconsin Writers award for short fiction.

**Letizia,** the little girl who refused to write, refused to do anything, until I said, "Write to me. Tell me what you're so mad about." She grinned and started writing as if her pencil was on fire.

**Stephen Boehrer,** the married priest who had so much to say that he wrote four novels including the award-winning *The Purple Culture.*

**Roses** (her dad gave her an extra "s"), a retired teacher, mother of seven, who decided photographs cost too much and started sketching what she saw on her travels. She brought the sketches to workshops, wrote her memories, and had them bound in a spiral sketchbook. The last time I heard from her, she said she has Alzheimer's and can no longer write like that, but she was grateful that she had her book and wrote her memories while she could.

One day I'll write a play with these people and more as characters. It will star a gorgeous version of me and also: the horror writer whose stories frightened me, the shy little woman who wrote the most surprising erotica, the political activist, the conservative lawyer, the Jewish woman who was torn from her family in Munich in 1939, and the German woman who remembered being so proud when her daddy finally got a job and her mom sewed the swastika on his new uniform. These people taught me to write. In my struggle to help them, I came up with techniques I never would have thought of if I had worked with only my own writing. I'll put what I can in this book and hope it turns out like Pam Parker's dream. We'll attend the signings together and she can buy my book and I'll buy hers. She wrote the first pages of her novel, *Katya,* in one of my classes, so I get credit for that, too.

*Follow your dreams!*

*Judy*

# Chapter One

# OH, YES YOU CAN

It's none of their business that you have to learn how to write. Let them think you were born that way.

—Ernest Hemingway, novelist, short story writer

## Ah, If Only . . .

A year of solitude. The perfect computer. A great education. A supportive family. A bottomless well of talent and ideas. A line of publishers with checkbooks in hand.

Not gonna happen? Well, then what?

This is where the coach looks over the top of her glasses and says, "You want to write? What's stopping you?" And you say:

- Too busy

- No inspiration

- People interrupt

- I need a new computer/workspace/coffeepot

- I have writer's block

A ten-year-old visited my studio with her mom. The little girl looked around at all the books and said that she used to be a writer, but lately, oh—fingertips to forehead—she was suffering a dreadful writer's block. Her career was in ruins. I showed her my block—a stack of toy alphabet blocks glued together by a friend who was either sympathetic or just plain sick of listening to me. The stack spells out "JUDY'S WRITER'S BLOCK," and it sits high on my bookshelf. I can see it when I look over the top of my glasses.

We all have blocks of one sort or another. Real writers write anyway.

## Myths about Writers

I think most of our barriers stem from myths we believe about writers—that they put fingers on the keyboard and words roll out, easily and quickly. The Muse wakes them in the morning. They are prolific and naturally, massively, talented.

Of all the myths about writers, the most defeating is the belief that you need to have natural talent, that the ability to write is a mystical gift given to a few lucky people who live in the sunlight, no hard work needed—that you either get the gift or not, and if not, you may as well forget about trying. But when you think about it, we all know plenty of people who are talented and clever and still do not achieve their goals. They want to write (or dance or play the violin), but they never really make it happen.

You can.

## What It Takes to Write Well

In the studio, there are three, fourteen-foot-long shelves full of books written by Redbird writers and friends. I know and love the authors of these books, and here's what I can tell you about them. They work hard. They are interesting people who lead the same kind of lives as the rest of us and have the same problems. The difference is that they do what it takes. And what it takes is:

- Commitment
- Confidence
- Courage
- Communication
- Craft

## Commitment

One of the books on that shelf belongs to Doug Jacobson. Doug is a business-man, husband, dad, and grandfather. He obviously has a few things to do with his time, but he had an idea for a World War II novel, did heavy research, and gave it a try. When I read the manuscript, I took him at his word that he really wanted my opinion and said, "Are you willing to put two more years into this?"

He took a deep breath, pulled out his checkbook, and registered to attend the Shut Up & Write! workshop. He reminded me of that conversation a few years—and a few rewrites—later, when he stood in Harry W. Schwartz Bookshop in Milwaukee signing copies of his debut novel, *Night of Flames*.

There is nothing more important than commitment. It beats out talent, brains, and friends in high places—all of which you can have and waste. In order to write, you have to put your butt in the chair and your fingers on the keyboard and make words until you have a long string of them, then you rewrite, then you edit.

There's no point in wondering if you are a writer or talking about what you are going to write—you just have to do it. You have to commit to the process. Commitment makes you hold on, learn what you need to learn, put in the hours, and try again. And the best thing about it is that it's not a gift. It's something you can get for yourself.

## Confidence

This isn't egotism. When egotists ask for feedback, they listen for compliments and dismiss critiques. If they don't hear high praise, they'll walk out of the writing group and complain about the other participants. When confident writers ask for feedback, they listen for ideas they can use. They know they own the writing; it is theirs to adjust or improve or keep just the way it is. They own the good and the bad of it. That's confidence.

## Courage

It takes courage to write with the kind of gut-level honesty that makes for good writing. When you write deeply, it makes you vulnerable. You don't know for sure what people will say about you or your writing, so it takes courage to put it out there. This does get a little easier with experience, but the truth is, if you are a writer who cares—which is the very best kind—you may always be a little nervous when you write and when you open those pages to others. You just do it anyway. That's courage.

## Communication

If I had only one rule to live by, it would be this: Write to communicate, not to impress. My bulging file on the topic of communication contains a dog-eared poster:

> Jesus said to them: "Who do you say that I am?"
>
> And they replied: "You are the eschatological manifestation of the ground of our being; the kerygma in which we find the ultimate meaning of our interpersonal relationship."
>
> And Jesus said: "What???"

I'm with Jesus on this one. I hate it when people try to sound fancy. I see strength in plain, simple language. In an essay that appeared in *Ms. Magazine*, Alice Walker describes her mother as a woman "with a look that could make you sit down." Nine simple words, that's all, and you not only see Walker's mother, you hear yourself saying, "Yes, ma'am."

## Craft

My big sister used to play the violin, or thought she did. Mostly she chased me around the house making horrid screechy noises. One night she had a dream that I died and they buried me in her violin, my little face barely visible behind the strings. That freaked her out enough to make her quit playing.

To play well, my sister would have had to study—the sounds, the music, how to tuck her chin and draw the bow. You don't just pick up a violin and make good music. You don't just pick up a pen and make good writing. There's no way around it; you have to practice. You have to study the craft.

## You Are Never Too Young, Never Too Old

Alice Raymond was raised in an orphanage. When she was in third grade, she wrote a story, and a boy in her class grabbed her paper and read it, out loud, to the other kids. They laughed, and she never wrote again until she was in her eighties.

The first time she read one of her pieces to me, she read so shyly I could hardly hear her. Two years later, with a lot of encouragement and pushing, she stood on a stage and read to an audience of 250 enthusiastic fans. When the applause died down, she turned to me and said, "This is the best day of my life!"

Alice kept writing and sold every copy printed of a small, handmade book of stories and poems about her life. When she died, at eighty-seven, I had the honor of reading her poem, "The Rogue," at the service celebrating her life.

## Oh. Yes. You. Can.

If you really want to write, you can do it. You can close your email, open a blank page, and put some words on it. You can take a notebook with you to the coffee shop, the doctor's office, the football game. You can learn the skills you need, and you can see your words in print.

Oh. Yes. You. Can.

## The Rogue
by Alice Raymond

A rogue rapped on my door last night,
The time, ten-past-two.
I impishly admitted him—
A daring thing to do.

He said, "My, you look exquisite
In head scarf and flannel gown."
Pleased, I smiled as I
Took my curlers down.

I offered him a cooling drink.
We each drained our cup.
He whispered to me hoarsely,
"Delicious Seven-Up."

I mutely asked the watching moon,
"Well, what is it you think?"
You won't believe it,
But I saw the fellow wink.

(Please, angels, help me
With this villain and his scheming.)
He touched my withered cheek and said,
"Goodbye, my dear, you're dreaming."

# Chapter Two

# IN A NUTSHELL
## The Writer's Process

I think I did pretty well, considering I started out with nothing but a bunch of blank paper.

—Steve Martin, actor, comedian, writer

WRITERS HAVE VERY DIFFERENT WORK HABITS. Some write every day, others only on deadline. Some use outlines, others wing it. Some write slowly and deliberately, others slap dash to the finish line and then rewrite. Some rewrite easily, others fight it every step of the way. A lot depends on how our brains are wired, but if you could blend all the habits into an ideal pattern, you would:

- Write every day
- Get an idea
- Mull it over
- Try some preliminary scribbles
- Decide if it is a story or information
- Organize your thoughts
- Do a warm-up exercise
- Write from the inside
- Revise and rewrite

- Edit

- Get published

- Go spend the big bucks

# The Ideal Pattern

## Write Every Day

Should you write every day? Sure.

Will you? Probably not.

In all these years, I've known only one writer who actually gets up at five every morning and writes for two hours before he goes to his day job. If you want to feel guilty all the time, promise yourself you'll start writing at five every morning. If you don't want to feel guilty, acknowledge that there are days and weeks when you're just not going to do it. Cut yourself some slack. Say, "My shoulder hurts," or "I'm tired of this." Set a date when you'll get started again and reassess if necessary. You make the decision. That way you don't need to feel guilty or put upon. You are in control.

When it's time to start again, set a goal you can reach. In *The Artist's Way*, Julia Cameron says to write three pages a day. That's a decent goal. If you're having a good week, write three perfect pages a day. If the dogs are barking, write three lousy pages. Do whatever you have to do to meet your three-page goal, and count everything—drafts, journals, emails, reports, and letters to the editor. Write bigger if you have to. Use wider margins or smaller sheets of paper. Just make sure you write three pages.

When you write three pages a day, you keep the system oiled. You get used to making words, to crafting your thoughts into sentences, to feeling the "ink" flow. For example: I'm an on-again/off-again writer, so I make sure I write three pages a day the week before I start a project. The first pages are pathetic, but by the time I need to get serious, I'm warmed up and writing better.

The important thing is to make a habit of writing as much as you say you will. It doesn't have to be wonderful, it just has to be writing.

## Get an Idea

A former Dutch spy told novelist Shauna Singh Baldwin she should write the story of Noor, an Indo-American woman who served as a spy in Nazi-occupied France during the Second World War. Shauna was busy with another book, so she put the idea on the back burner for a few years. Eventually she started wondering how it feels to be a racially and culturally hybrid person in a war zone. That wondering led to several years of research and the writing of the Canadian Giller Prize finalist, *The Tiger Claw*.

If you are like most writers, you have more ideas than you have time to write. If not, look to your bookshelves or magazine rack for clues. You will do your best if you write the type of thing you like to read. Why? Because you know so much about it—length, topics, tone, what's been said way too often, and what hasn't been said often enough.

Find a book that lists story starters. Thumb through a newspaper for headlines that set your imagination rolling. Rifle through your idea box. Don't have an idea box? Start one. Use any kind of box. Keep it handy, and fill it with clippings, photos, toys, scraps of wallpaper, anything that stirs you.

When it's time to start working, focus on an idea that calls to you, one that's just a little more appealing than the others. Don't get too serious about the decision just yet. This is a flirtation, not a wedding.

## Mull It Over

Live with the idea for a few days. Let it soak into you. Let your imagination play around in it. Run a few phrases in your head. Imagine it printed . . . where? In a magazine? A collection of short stories? A letter to your kids? A how-to book for CEOs?

Or maybe you see it as private writing, just for you. Are there people in it? What are they like? Is there a setting? Have you ever been there? Would you need to do a lot of research? Would you enjoy doing the research? Is the information available to you?

If a character stays in your head or your idea still attracts you after a few days, you're on to something.

## Try Some Preliminary Scribbles

Preliminary scribbles are "sloppy copy" writing. Take a few of the thoughts you had in the "mull-it-over" phase and put them on paper. No need to be fancy or even accurate—you are just seeing how things feel to you. Does the idea hold your interest? If you hope to write a book of either fiction or nonfiction, you will have to live with the characters or topic for a long time. Do you think you can do that? Is the idea big enough for a fully dimensional story, or is it merely an anecdote? Does your imagination fill with possibilities? Do the preliminary scribbles get you excited about writing more?

## Decide: Story or Information?

Once upon a time the writing world was divided into two categories, fiction and nonfiction. College programs, how-to books, and seminars were devoted to one or the other. There were subcategories like "novels" and "articles," but basically writing was either make-believe or factual, fiction or nonfiction, and you approached the process accordingly. Fiction was filled with characters. Nonfiction was filled with information. The fiction writer daydreamed. The nonfiction writer got down to business. It was luscious creativity versus dry bones. Zero paycheck versus food on the table.

The trouble with this two-party system is that it's confusing. If you want to write about your life or the lives of others, you stand at the crossroads between fiction and nonfiction, or at least you did until the advent of New Journalism and Creative Nonfiction. Then, finally, there was a home for those who use the techniques of fiction to write true stories.

But even with that, we have confusion in the language. The term "story" is used to mean everything from literary fiction to newspaper articles. You'd think that as wordsmiths we'd do a better job of smithing.

There is a simpler way to look at things. If we re-divide the world of writing into "story" and "information," we have a cleaner, more natural way to approach both the writing and the marketing. Stories—real or imagined—are created, organized, written, and marketed in one way. Informational works are created, organized, written, and marketed in another.

To create a story, you reach deep in your belly to find the narrative drive and the scenes that push it forward.

To write an informational piece, you plan a logical, easy-to-understand placement of facts and supporting material.

You use characters (real or imagined) and scenes (real or imagined) in both forms. You also might include information with your story, or a story with your information—but the story rules in one case and the message rules in the other.

"Story" includes all things that have a narrative drive: novels, short stories, your grandfather's trip down the Amazon, and the day you fell out of the plum tree. You may include information, but the emphasis is on the story.

"Information" includes all things written to help people understand: letters, reports, articles, essays, profiles, or how-to books. You may include stories, but the emphasis is on the information.

## Organize Your Thoughts

Some writers say they start with an idea, one nugget or scene, and proceed through the writing like a train going through a dark tunnel with no view of what's ahead. Their characters take over; the authors go along for the ride. If this works for you, fine. But most writers find it easier to have at least a skeleton outline.

My favorite tools for creating bare-bones outlines, the Bubble Outline and the Alligator Outline, are both described later in this book. If you are writing a story (fiction or nonfiction, imagined or real), you can rough out a plot line using the Bubble Outline (Chapter Four). If you are writing an informational piece (an essay, article, or nonfiction book), you can use the Alligator Outline (Chapter Eight). Bubble and Alligator Outlines may look like kid's games, but they are extremely efficient ways to structure your work. When you have your thoughts organized, your imagination is free to do the writing.

## Do a Warm-up Exercise

If you've been writing three pages a day, you won't have to spend much time on warm-up. If not, write at least a few pages to loosen up and get your imagination and words flowing. Start with the words, *I love . . .* , *I hate . . .* , or *I wish . . .* , and write three pages.

Or take an object out of your idea box and write about it. Tell your truly accepting writing friend (mine is a stuffed gorilla named Alfred) why you chose this object or why it chose you. Write plainly and simply, as if you are writing a letter. Do it quickly. Don't lift your pen from the page. If the exercise starts feeling like the dumbest thing you ever did, write: "This is the dumbest thing I ever did, this is the dumbest thing I ever did, this is the dumbest thing I ever did . . ." until your imagination (or impatience) moves you off the dime. The point is to make words, not sense.

## Write from the Inside

"Write from the inside" has two meanings. You write from the inside of you, and you write from the inside of a scene. When you combine the two "insides," you write naturally and powerfully.

### Writing from Inside of You

The best writing comes from deep in your belly. It's powerful. You can feel the liver and the heartbeat. At this point, the writing is between you and the page. It's intimate. You give your life to it. You stuff the idea, the characters, the setting, the action, and your memories and imagination into your belly. Let it enter your bloodstream and flow through your fingers onto the page.

### Writing from Inside of a Scene

This approach to writing uses your imagination and all the knowledge you've collected over the years to write a vivid scene. You select a scene from your rough outline, decide on a point of view, envision yourself entering the scene, and use your deep imagination to spur the writing.

## Revise and Rewrite

The revision process includes early rewrites, feedback, re-keying, letting it sit, and then doing more rewrites. People use different labels for the steps, but the process is similar.

*Early Rewrites*

Reread your work and fix what you think needs fixing before you show it to anyone. Don't marry the text at this point, just try to feel the tone and flow, and look for obvious clinkers. If you would like a barometer of how much time other people spend doing this, I can tell you that it's common for me to rewrite the same paragraph ten or twelve times. Other writers see few errors in their drafts and do more of the fixing later, after they get feedback.

*Get Feedback*

This is where your writing group steps in. These are the wise people who struggle as you do to make music of the written word. They can spot a wobbly point of view. They wonder if this story might be better written in first person. They find civilized ways to make suggestions and you find civilized ways to respond. Do you love them? Not always. But you need them.

*Re-key*

This means literally re-type, re-enter, or re-key the words. Put the hard copy next to your keyboard, use what you want from it, but re-enter the entire manuscript, fixing and changing as you go.

"Why?" Because this way it will get better, faster.

"Can't I just cut-and-paste?" Yes, but it's a question of time and quality. Writers who take the time to re-key get to the finals faster, with more grace. When you re-key, you change something on page three that causes a shift on page six, and that in turn causes an exciting development on page ten. You go deeper into your words and into the story or topic.

You get to skip re-keying if you are writing on the firing line. Reporters working on breaking stories and students writing exams do not have time to re-key. They barely have time to write.

*Let It Sit*

A manuscript is like bread dough: it needs to rest and rise. Give it some time after the heat of writing the first drafts before processing the feedback and re-keying. If you can, wait until you forget exact phrases—a day, a week, a month. Wait until you can read a passage and see what you left out, what was in your mind that didn't make it onto paper. Wait until you have had time to think about the feedback. Then go on to the next step.

### Rewrite More

A while ago, I saw a television interview with a curmudgeonly guy whose book had just been released. When asked about his writing process and revisions, he pointed to a stack of paper taller than his desk. "That's the draft." There were more pages, but he'd trashed them. We rewrite and rewrite and rewrite until we're sick of it, or hit the deadline, or decide it's really, really, good.

## Edit

I know one writer who sold her first story with a handwritten, poorly edited manuscript. For her sake, I wish the magazine hadn't taken it, because from then on, the writer thought that was the way to go. "It's the editor's job to fix things." She never sold another story.

Pay attention to the niceties. Grammar. Spelling. Usage. If you are not good at editing—and a surprising number of authors are not—get help from a pro.

It's your job to get a copy of the agent/editor/publisher guidelines and prepare your manuscript to the exact specifications. You can get imperious after you're famous. Until then, it's best to play by the rules.

## Get Published

Not everyone is anxious to be published. One excellent writer, when asked if she planned to submit a particular piece, said, "But what if they take it?" She felt as if it would no longer be hers, that she'd be giving up something very precious. However, for most people, getting published is the point.

When you make the first, fifth, or fiftieth sale or you win an award, you can let go of the rejections that upset you. You papered the bathroom walls with those, stabbed them onto your grandfather's memo spindle, burned them over black candles. Now it's Happy Time. What a thrill! A little disconcerting, too, if too much is edited or you don't like the artwork. Still, you are published—right there in black and white or colored pixels. Call everyone you know. Put the news on your blog or on Facebook. Send emails to those you barely know or rarely see. Revel in the glory. You deserve it.

## Go Spend the Big Bucks

Here is the hierarchy of earnings. With some exceptions, poetry earns the least. The next steps up on the fiscal ladder are: short stories, story collections, novels, technical writing, reporting, public relations, speeches, and higher level corporate work. Authors of best sellers are on a different ladder entirely. You can tell who they are by looking at the book cover. Their names are on top, over the titles.

Now let's talk status. To see who gets the most respect in the field, you can pretty much flip the ladder. Novelists are on top. Poets and short fiction writers are slightly below, and the corporate writers, especially tech writers, are near the bottom. Tech writers tend to apologize, "I just write manuals." They should not apologize. They should count how many big-time writers started out doing technical writing. That's where they learned to communicate, to pull the threads together, to meet the deadline.

# Do It All Over Again

Few things are as exciting as knowing that the thing you created—the painting, the play, the lullaby—gives pleasure to people. When you sit in an audience and hear actors reading your lines, when you see your book on the shelf, when you go back and read what you've written and truly, truly like it, you are hooked.

No question about it. You will face that blank page and do it all over again.

# CHAPTER THREE

# CHARACTERS
## Real and Imagined

The personages in a tale shall be alive, except in the case of corpses, and always the reader shall be able to tell the corpses from the other.

—Mark Twain, humorist

I took a clean white piece of paper—like a sheet freshly ironed for making love—and rolled it into the carriage. I wrote my name, and immediately the words began to flow, one thing linked to another and another. Characters stepped from the shadows, each with a face, a voice, passions and obsessions.

Isabel Allende, novelist

CHARACTERS ARE AT THE HEART OF WRITING. Whether people or parrots, real or imagined, alive or dead, principals in novels or case histories in how-to books, characters are the prime drivers of the written word. They make readers want to read your work to find out what happened.

We tend to think of "characters" in the fictional sense, made-up people like Scarlett O'Hara or Harry Potter. But we also write about nonfiction characters—people who exist, or did exist, somewhere in this world, living and breathing pretty much as they seem on paper. Bob Dylan, Eleanor Roosevelt, and the relatives in your memoir are all nonfiction characters.

Whether you are writing fiction or nonfiction, you'll save yourself a lot of time and trouble if you get to know your characters before you begin to write. Take your basic ideas or memories and flesh them out to the point where the characters seem fully alive to you, so you know how they look, sound, feel, taste, and smell. When you can imagine them sitting across the table or dancing in the moonlight, you are ready to write.

## The Character Wheel

My favorite tool for fleshing out real or imaginary characters is the Character Wheel. It grew out of workshops in which I struggled to find a simple, creative way to use sensual details to help writers develop characters and bring them to life (see Figure 1).

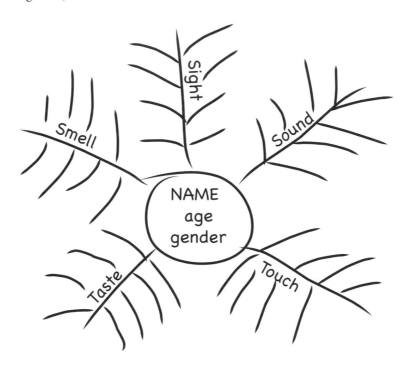

Figure 1. The Character Wheel

In using a Character Wheel, you work with the five senses: sight, sound, touch, taste, and smell. You can use a sheet of blank paper or a wall-sized whiteboard. Within minutes, you have your character clear enough in your mind to begin writing. If you create the wheel on paper, you can hang it on the wall next to your computer where you can see at a glance whether your character's eyes are blue or brown, whether it's the right or left leg that's shorter than the other one, whether those fingernails are sequined or painted green.

To create a Character Wheel, draw a circle in the center of a blank piece of paper or whiteboard. In this circle, write the name, age, and gender of your character.

Next draw five spokes extending out from the circle: one each at twelve, two, five, seven, and ten o'clock.

Label the spokes Sight, Sound, Touch, Taste, and Smell.

Now draw a bunch of short lines off each spoke. On the short lines, you are going to note details about the character, using one or two word phrases—just enough to jog your memory.

## Creating Kelly

In workshops, I draw the wheel on a whiteboard. First, I draw the circle and spokes. Then someone comes up with a name: "Kelly." I ask another person for an age: "23," and yet another person for the gender: "female." Sometimes the name and gender match; sometimes they don't. We take what comes.

From there we go to the senses, moving around the wheel, jotting down ideas related to sight, sound, touch, taste, and smell. This is a brainstorming session— all ideas are welcomed, none is questioned. Move quickly. Don't worry about whether things make sense or fit together; you can fix that later, and who knows, maybe your wild, wacky imagination will come up with just the perfect thing to create an unforgettable character.

I write every idea on the board, one after another, until we make it around the wheel, and, *voila*, a brand-new character comes to life (see Figure 2).

### The Hub

Name:      KELLY

Age:        23

Gender:    female

### Spokes on the Wheel

*Sight*

What do you see when you imagine Kelly?

Tall. Blonde. Blue eyes. Thin. Muscled. Water bottle. Yellow shorts.

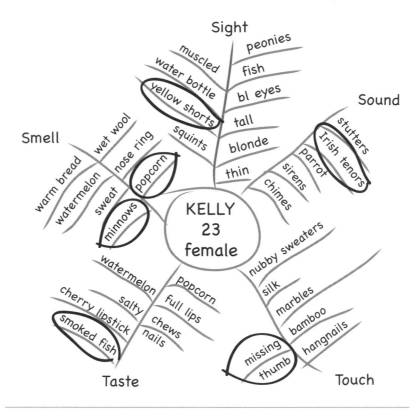

Figure 2.  Character Wheel for Kelly

What does Kelly like to look at?

Fish. Peonies.

Anything else related to sight or eyes?

Squints.

### Sound

What do you hear when you listen to Kelly?

Stutters.

What does Kelly like the sound of?

Irish tenors. Her parrot Isaac.

Anything else related to sound or ears?

Sirens. Clock chimes.

*Touch*

What does Kelly feel like? (Note: this is tactile, not emotional.)

Silky blouse. Nubby sweater.

What does Kelly like to touch?

Marbles. Bamboo.

Anything else related to touch or hands?

Hangnails. Missing thumb.

*Taste*

The last two senses—taste and smell—are often harder for people to imagine. But persevere; it's worth it for the richness these details will bring to your writing. Think of taste as the power of lemons: juicy, tart, squirts. Can you read that without having your mouth water?

What does Kelly taste like?

Watermelon. Salty. Cherry lipstick.

What does she like the taste of?

Smoked fish. Popcorn.

Anything else related to taste or mouth?

Full lips. Chews nails.

*Smell*

If taste is the power of lemons, smell is the power of popcorn.

What does Kelly smell like?

Watermelon. Warm bread. Sweat.

What does she like the smell of?

Minnows. Wet wool. Popcorn.

Anything else related to smell or nose?

Nose ring.

## Circle the Missing Thumb

On each of the sensory spokes, find and circle at least one characteristic that is unexpected—a detail that doesn't quite fit with the others. If you don't see an unexpected detail, invent one. This is how you ensure that your character is fresh and interesting, and not stereotypical.

The character Kelly was pretty stereotypical until one writer said, "She's missing the thumb on her right hand." Wow! Think what happens when a character is missing the thumb on her right hand. The missing thumb becomes an element in the story. This new person either sits on her hand or shows it proudly, shakes hands with strangers or holds back, talks about it or keeps the story hidden. The missing thumb adds new dimensions and makes her a more memorable character.

Real characters are also full of surprises. Think about your favorite uncle, or maybe the one you try to avoid. Go around the wheel: Sight, Sound, Touch, Taste, Smell. What do you notice or try to ignore about him? My great-grandfather had a glass eye. I never knew which one because as a kid, I was afraid to look at him. If I used him as a model for a character, you can bet someone in the story, perhaps a little girl, would do everything she could to avoid looking him square in his not-real eye.

# Creating Major Characters

To flesh out a main character for a lengthy piece such as a biography or novel, get as many details down on the page as you can. The wheel will look like chicken scratch and that's just fine. Make no attempt to be tidy—just write an abundance of one- or two-word clues to the character. When the character walks off the page and starts talking to you, you have enough.

Griffin Peake is the main character in a novel written by workshop participant David Howard. Here is a sampling of David's first ideas about Griffin, followed by an excerpt from a draft of the novel (see Figure 3).

## Creating Griffin

### The Hub

Name:      GRIFFIN

Age:       15

Gender:    male

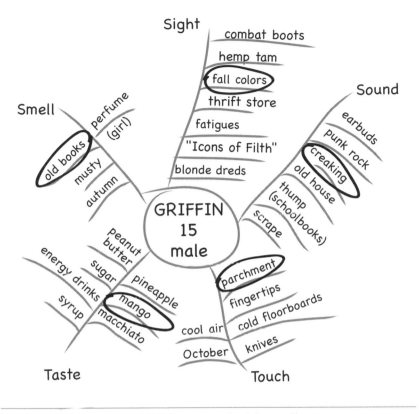

Figure 3.  Character Wheel for Griffin

## Spokes on the Wheel

### Sight

Combat boots. Hemp tam. Fall colors. Thrift store. Fatigues.
"Icons of Filth" T-shirt. Blonde dreadlocks.

### Sound

Earbuds. Punk rock. Creaking. Old house. Thump of schoolbooks.
Scrape of metal chairs.

### Touch

Parchment. Fingertips. Cold floorboards. Knives. Cool air.
October in Wisconsin.

*Taste*

Peanut butter. Sugar. Energy drinks. Syrup. Pineapple. Mango. Macchiato.

*Smell*

Perfumed girl. Old books. Musty. Autumn.

David could add enough details to fill a large whiteboard, but this is enough to get started. Notice the amount of sensual detail in this passage, how David uses the cool air on Griffin's skin and the knots in his shoulder muscles to bring the reader close to his subject.

> Griffin awoke from deep, troubled sleep. For a few minutes he lay in bed, feeling the cool air on his skin and staring at the sunlight slanting across the ceiling of his room. Silence lay thick and full upon the house. Then the alarm clicked on, and he stretched to shut it off. He freed his legs from the twisted sheets and pulled himself out of bed, yawning and massaging his cramped arms. God. The nightmares were back. No fun dreams about hot girls. Another night of fear and darkness. He shook it off and got out of bed.
>
> Under the shower, he worked out the knots in his shoulder muscles, toweled off, scowled at his complexion in the mirror, fussed with his teeth and face and all that. He didn't even worry about his hair; that routine took basically forever. Griffin would have bet that when he washed, dried, twisted and waxed his dreads, he spent more time on his hair than most girls did. But then, he only did it one night a week.

## Creating Minor Characters

Jacky Smith is a fictitious character created by Annie Chase, who worked on many of the examples in this book. Jacky is not a main character, so Annie didn't need to create a comprehensive wheel—just enough to make him come alive in her imagination (see Figure 4).

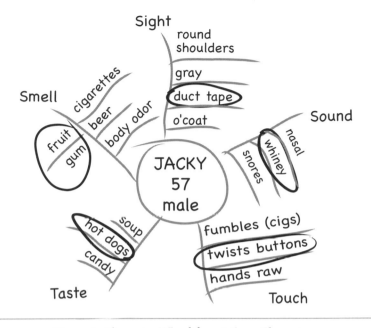

Figure 4. Character Wheel for a Minor Character

## Creating a Minor Character—Jacky

### The Hub

Name:      JACKY

Age:        57

Gender:    male

### Spokes on the Wheel

*Sight*

Round shoulders. Wispy gray hair. Duct tape on his shoes.
Ill-fitting overcoat.

*Sound*

Nasal voice. Whiney. Snores while sitting on bus stop bench.

*Touch*

Fumbles for cigarettes. Twists coat buttons. Hands raw.

*Taste*

Eats at soup kitchen. Likes 3/$1 gas station hot dogs. Candy.

*Smell*

Cigarettes. Beer. Body odor. Fruit gum.

After Annie circled the unexpected items—duct tape, whiney, twists buttons, hot dogs, fruit gum—on the chart, Jacky came to life for her. She stopped adding details and started writing.

> The November wind was bitter, in spite of the thin sunshine, and it swept into the open side of the bus shelter. Jacky pulled his baggy over-coat tighter around his body. He craned his neck to squint up at the clock tower. It was nearly eleven o'clock, time to head toward St. Ben's for the free lunch the church handed out. He got up and began to walk, his broken shoe flapping with each step. Maybe there would be a baloney sandwich to go with the soup today, he thought hopefully.

Notice how Annie uses sensual details to show Jacky and his world so intimately that you are there with him, feeling the bitter wind and the rhythm of his flapping shoe. This is natural writing—the kind that happens when you take time to develop a character in a concrete, sense-based, way. After just a few minutes of noting details on the wheel, you know your character so well that when you put him out in the cold at the bus stop, you see and feel it clearly and can share that with your readers.

The wheel works as well for nonfiction characters. Had Jacky been real rather than imagined, Annie would have noticed if she was thin on detail or where she might want to do some checking to fill in the gaps. You don't have to use every detail you have, but every detail you do not have is a lost opportunity.

## When You Write about Real People

The next example involves a nonfiction character, my grandmother, who was the centerpiece in an essay I wrote about older people fighting to stay out of nursing homes. I thought I knew every line in her face until I started creating a Character Wheel and forced myself to move step by step through the senses, remembering details. Bringing specifics to the surface, both on paper and in my mind, gave me more to work with when I started writing (see Figure 5).

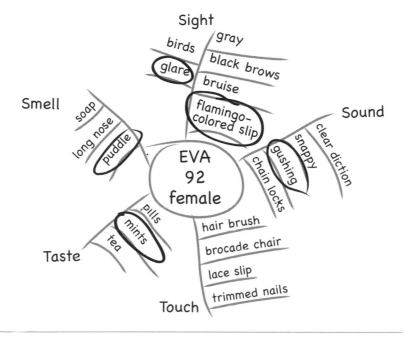

Figure 5.  Character Wheel for Eva

## Remembering Eva

### The Hub

| | |
|---|---|
| Name: | EVA |
| Age: | 92 |
| Gender: | female |

### Spokes on the Wheel

*Sight*

Gray braids. Black brows. Bruise. Flamingo-colored lace slip.
Birds. Glare.

*Sound*

Clear diction. Snappy. Gushing. Chain locks on doors.

*Touch*

Hair brush. Brocade chair. Lace slip. Trimmed nails.

*Taste*

Pills. Tea. Mints.

*Smell*

Soap. Long nose. Puddle.

This is the beginning of the essay I wrote. It appeared in the Sunday magazine of *The Milwaukee Journal* under the title, "The Price of Independence: At 92, Eva holds tightly to her own way of life."

> Eva stands in the hosiery aisle at Woolworth's, shaking with anger. She glares at the baby-faced clerk like an eagle ready to attack. Suddenly the lines on her old face rearrange into a horrified look. There is a gushing sound. Her white summer shoes fill with the product of an irritated colon.
>
> After a stunned silence, Eva lifts her shoulders, steps out of the reeking puddle and hurries from the store.
>
> She lies to protect herself. "The doctor gave me the wrong cathartic."
> The lie is almost convincing.
>
> "People like that uppity clerk think I'm feebleminded just because I'm old," she says to her younger companion. "Well, I have news for them. I'm not ready for the fox farm yet!"
>
> "The Price of Independence" by Judy Bridges
> *The Milwaukee Journal,* November 28, 1982

The lead of this essay raises some ethical questions that I discuss later in this chapter, in the section "Writing about Friends and Family?" At this point, what I'd like you to notice is that Eva "glares at the baby-faced clerk like an eagle ready to attack." I'd forgotten about that glare until I put her characteristics on the wheel, but the minute I wrote it down, I knew I'd never forget again.

## Tips for Using the Character Wheel

### Practice

Create at least two Character Wheels: one for an imaginary character, another for someone you know. Set a timer for fifteen minutes each. Moving quickly opens doors that may surprise you.

## Create a Wheel for Each Character

Create a fully developed wheel for each major character. Include several items on each spoke and circle unexpected details. Less developed wheels will do for minor characters. In all cases, keep adding details until the character comes alive for you.

## Keep Your Notes Short

One or two words should be enough. All you need is a reminder; your imagination will do the rest.

## Stay with Concrete, Sensual Details

Later, when you're writing, you will use these concrete details to illuminate the deeper psychological aspects of your character. Straight shoulders show pride. Flamingo-colored lace shows a touch of sauciness and maybe an interesting history.

## Notice Any Spokes that Are Regularly Light

Chances are these are the senses that you tend to write lightly as well, which means you have an opportunity to beef up your writing by focusing more in these areas.

Author Sara Vogan, my all-time favorite writing teacher, went through her drafts with five colored pencils, one for each sense, and circled the sense references as she came upon them. If she was light on any one color, she knew she had an opportunity to do better. When I do this, I am routinely light on blue for sound, and the truth is that my hearing has never been particularly acute—I have to pay close attention to hear sounds and even closer attention to write about them. When I see a lack of blue on the page, I see an opportunity to improve my writing.

## Aim for Simplicity

It's difficult to hit the right balance between adding details and overdoing them. There is no absolute rule for this, no exact number of things to say. Earlier I mentioned Alice Walker's description of her mother having "a look that would make you sit down." I adore that simplicity. But at other times, you might want to rewrite "Bob loved his '67 Mustang" to "Behind the wheel of his '67 muscle car, Bob felt intensely alive. When he pressed his foot on the throttle, the adrenaline flowed and his blood raced along with the well-tuned engine."

It's a matter of taste and practice—and to use the Irish vernacular, there's "nothing for it" but to keep writing until it sounds right.

## Play "Twenty Questions"

Writers' magazines often include articles that feature exercises you can use to discover deep psychological aspects of your characters, such as writing their resumes or answering lists of questions about their backgrounds, lifestyles, wins, losses, and miseries. The longest list of questions I've seen is seventeen pages. I never used it, but if I did, I would know what time my character goes to bed at night and whether she brushes her teeth straight up and down or sideways.

Novelist Elaine Bergstrom distributes a list of twenty questions to participants in her workshops. Answering the questions allows you to delve deeper into the psychology of your character without forcing you to write more pages than you can keep track of (see Figure 6).

## Keep a Binder

Place copies of your Character Wheels in a binder. Add photos of people who look like your characters, plus bits of background or dialogue you write in the middle of the night or while you're hanging out in the coffee shop. Novelist Stephen Boehrer fills a binder with information about his characters, including magazine photos of clothing styles and colors. When he needs to bring a character to mind, he has only to open the binder and thumb through the pages.

# Tips for Working with Characters

## Choose Characters Wisely

Novelist Shauna Singh Baldwin says, "Before you settle in to writing a novel about particular characters, make sure you like them." It can take two to five years to write a novel. During that time, you will be intensely involved with the

# Playing Twenty Questions with Your Character
## by Elaine Bergstrom

1.  What does s/he look like?

2.  When and where was s/he born and raised?

3.  Siblings or an only child? If siblings, how did they get along?

4.  What kind of family life did s/he have?

5.  What kind of religious life?

6.  Education level?

7.  A good student or a poor one? Class leader or follower?

8.  Outgoing or introvert?

9.  How was adolescence? Sexually active or withdrawn?

10. What sort of speech or physical mannerisms does your character have?

11. Name three defining moments in your character's life before your story begins. If these were minor moments and the story is going to be the major event, give the minor ones and show how the seeds of her/his reaction color the present situation.

12. What does your character hate most about her/himself?

13. What are your character's main flaws? Does s/he realize they are flaws?

14. How does your character react under stress? Take charge? Weepy? Cowardly? Silly? If you're still not sure, write a stressful scene and see how s/he reacts.

15. How does your character react to boredom?

16. Name your character's greatest fear. Watch out for this. If you try to use it in the story and don't do it well, the result can be transparent.

17. If your character is good, what makes him/her good?

18. If your character is bad, what caused it? (Yes, just being born is an answer.)

19. How does s/he view the other characters in the story?

20. How do they view him/her?

Figure 6.  Playing Twenty Questions with Your Character by Elaine Bergstrom

characters, living their traumas, seeing and feeling the world through their bodies and minds. That's entirely too much time to spend with people you don't like.

## Choose Names Wisely

Give your characters names that look different on the page. After the first few pages, readers skim lines of attribution, noticing only the first few letters and the length and shape of names. Julie looks like Judy; Kevin looks like Keith. Readers have to concentrate to sort out who's who, which takes them away (momentarily) from the meaning of the writing. Choose names with different first letters, syllables, and even shapes—Julie and Annika, Kevin and Excelsior, Hank and Joshua.

## Just Say "Said"

Not long ago I walked past the door of a fourth-grade classroom and heard the teacher telling students to write "uttered" or "muttered" instead of "said." I almost rushed in to yell, "No! And don't tell them to write, 'He chimed,' either!" Honestly, did you ever hear a person *chime*?

You can—should—describe the manner in which a person said something if it adds information—if, for instance, he screamed, or spat, or choked out the words. Otherwise, "Jonas said" is quite enough.

In his novel *The Vicar of Wakefield*, Oliver Goldsmith consistently used "cried" instead of "said."

"'You cannot be ignorant, my children,' cried I."

We can forgive Goldsmith because he was writing in 1747. If he wrote that today, would you stick with him through thirty-two chapters of "I crieds"?

If the reader can tell who said what in a string of dialogue, you can skip the attribution altogether. When I know Jonas said it, you don't need to tell me.

## Avoid Overly Chatty, Overly Described Dialogue

Here's an example of overly chatty, overly described dialogue.

> "Why don't we meet for lunch today?" Chris suggested.
> "Just let me check my schedule to see if I have a meeting . . . hang on . . . where'd I put my calendar," Joan muttered. "Oh yes, here it is! How did it get over here in this drawer?" she grumbled.

"I had a client cancel, so I have an extra hour," Chris added.

"Yes, I can make it. Let's meet at the Thai buffet!" Joan exclaimed.

"Ooh, I love that place!" Chris cried. "See you at twelve-thirty?" she asked.

Here's an example of what happens when you rewrite the overly chatty, overly described dialogue to eliminate extraneous phrases and distracting attributions.

"Why don't we meet for lunch today," said Chris. "I had a client cancel, so I have an extra hour."

"Just let me check my calendar. I'm always misplacing that thing," said Joan. "Oh, here it is. Yes, I can make it. How about Thai Buffet?"

"I love that place," Chris said. "See you at twelve-thirty?"

In the following dialogue, each line moves the story along and brings you closer to the characters.

He could hear his heart thundering in his chest and the idea of Jiffy just standing there, for Christ's sake, was totally freaking him out. He cursed loud music and gunfire and city traffic for his hearing loss. His right ear was working overtime, he could almost feel it trying to reach out toward the edge of the tent to figure out what was going on and let him know. Another step. He bolted out.

There stood Jiffy, cane in hand, looking startled. "Hey," he said, face pale in the flashlight beam.

"What the hell are you doing?" Craig shouted.

"Taking a walk."

"Around my god damn tent?"

"Hey, no need to get upset, man, I was just walking around. Am I keeping you awake?"

"Listen, why can't you walk over there," Craig said, swinging the flashlight, "or there?"

"Because I need a starting point. I need something to walk around, Craig, I can't just walk back and forth."

"So walk around your fucking trailer."

"I do that all the time. I am lacking in purpose, I believe."

"What? Listen, if you don't stop it I'm going to just pack my tent and go to a hotel."

"I don't believe there's a hotel until you get to the next county, and that one's probably sold out."

> Craig did not like the sound of that.
> Jiffy eyed his cooler.
> "What? You want a beer?" he asked.
> "If you wouldn't mind," Jiffy said.
>
> —From *The Pilgrim's Ground* by Laurel Landis

## Writing about Friends and Family?

If you plan to write about a person you know but modify him slightly, I suggest that you modify him more than slightly. It's bad enough having your relatives imagine that they are the characters in your stories; it's a lot worse if they know for sure. Humorist Erma Bombeck said she lost a friend for every story she wrote. Some weren't even in the stories; they just thought they were.

Writer Anne Lamott suggests that if a woman wants to write a character like her ex, she can spare herself some trouble by giving the character a teeny tiny you-know-what. The ex is not likely to insist that she was writing about him.

In "The Price of Independence," I used a very personal event in a woman's life to introduce a piece on the fight for independence in old age. I could have started with statistics: "X number of elderly people fear the move to nursing homes." Or a quote: "According to Dr. Wise, elderly people fight to stay in their homes." Both are fine ways to begin, but I wanted more out of it. More intensity. More feeling.

The old woman in the Independence story was my grandmother, Eva. It was because of her that I was interested in the issue in the first place and wanted to write about it. She put the passion in the story for me, and I thought she would do that for others. Obviously you have ethical questions to answer when you write something like this. Should you use a real person? Should you use someone you love? Should you show her in such embarrassing circumstances? You might decide otherwise, but my decision to use that particular scene was based on the piercing way it showed the conflict between infirmity and pride. I knew my grandmother would not be aware of the article by the time it was published, and that if she had known about it, she would have told me to "quit fussing around and write the damned thing!"

When the essay appeared in the newspaper's Sunday magazine, my sister's mother-in-law called her and said, "You have to read this." It took awhile, but when my sister finally got around to reading it, she said out loud, "This sounds just like Gram!" Then she looked at the byline. Well, wha'da'ya know.

Here's my rule: If you are writing about friends or family, don't whitewash. It doesn't work anyway; the reader can smell it a mile away. But don't set out to hurt people, either. In other words, if your ex actually had a teeny tiny you-know-what, find something else to write about.

## Writing about Yourself?

Think twice before casting yourself as the main character in either a fictional or true story. If you want to write a story about yourself or from your life, write it in first person, without pretending it happened to Megan or Maggie or Marlowe.

If you absolutely must write your own story in third person, create a new character of yourself, starting with a radically different body shape and color of hair. That might keep you from making the child-you too adorable or the adult-you too excusable. But for the record, readers are still likely to guess it's you. I once wrote a day-my-dog-died story in which I played a sweet little girl named Maggie. If it ever surfaces, I will simply die.

The best characters seem like they're real, whether or not they are. When I started reading this story, I thought it was about the author.

> I was in seventh grade that year, and my dream was to get my hair done at Sally's Beauty Shop so I would look like the town girls. I had turned last year's lunchbox into what I called my beauty box. It held the rusty scissors I used to cut my bangs, a bar of Ivory Soap wrapped in waxed paper, and my favorite belonging, a compact I found in one of the boxes up in the attic. The puff was missing and only a thin line of powder remained around the rim of the bottom tray, but the mirror was clear and the lid closed with a satisfying snap.
>
> —From "The Haircut" by Carol Wobig

After I read the story, I got to thinking, Wait a minute, I know this author, she lived in town! How much of this story is true and how much is not? I'll never know and that's fine, because it's none of my business. What is my business, as a reader, is to appreciate the exquisite way she put me into the life of a little girl who hid her girly treasures in last year's lunchbox and, like so many other little girls, wished she was like the townies.

When you write about yourself, you end up with a mix of truth and fiction anyway, because none of us has an infallible memory. When my grandmother was near her end and refusing to socialize, she said she'd rather just sit still and think about her life. Knowing her, I asked, "You mean, you're rewriting history?" She said yes, she knew enough now to make things better. Imagine the difference in the books she would have written at the ages of fifteen, and fifty, and ninety-four.

My next book will be a collection of family stories titled *You Drive. You're Too Drunk to Sing*. I will write it in first person and make sure to include the notice: "This book is full of lies."

# CHAPTER FOUR

# STORIES
## Fact or Fiction

A novel can educate to some extent. But first, a novel has to entertain—
that's the contract with the reader: you give me ten hours and I'll give you
a reason to turn every page.

—Barbara Kingsolver, novelist

Somebody gets into trouble, gets out of it again. People love that story.
They never get tired of it.

—Kurt Vonnegut, novelist

When in doubt, have two guys come through the door with guns.

—Raymond Chandler, novelist

FROM PARABLES TO ADVERTISING, NURSERY RHYMES TO NOVELS, we learn, change our
lives, and buy products because of the stories we hear. Sometimes things we don't
even think of as stories affect us. When one of my cousins gave up a successful
business to become a full-time fisherman, his wife said she knew exactly when he
decided. It was when his dad told a story about a man who gave up everything
to homestead in Alaska. As soon as the words left her father-in-law's mouth, she
knew their lives would never be the same.

We are influenced by stories about religious and political leaders, by novels
about wars and social circumstance, by children's picture books, folk tales, and
movies. From the stork's delivery to the *Danse Macabre*, we frame our lives in bits
of fiction. Why were you late for school? I bet you had an answer, and the answer
was a story. Was it a true story? Maybe yes, maybe no. But whether the story was
truth or fiction, it was important to tell it well.

## Short Story or Novel?

Sometimes a new writer is determined to write a full-length novel, first thing, with no prior experience or time spent developing the craft. That's a hard thing to do. It takes most experienced writers two to five years, sometimes longer, to write a novel. That's a long time to work only to find out you're not so good with dialogue, or at developing characters or plot.

When you begin with short stories, you not only learn while you're writing them, you can, if you're lucky, create a buzz around your writing. Novelist Sara Vogan spent two years polishing her first published short story. It won a Pushcart Prize and attracted the attention of literary agents from coast to coast. She was just getting out of grad school and in the enviable position of deciding which of several agents she liked best. When the movie rights to her first novel, *In Shelly's Leg*, were optioned, she said that given the frugal way she had learned to live, the check would last her for years. She went from short story to full-time novelist in less than five years.

To write stories, short or long, fact or fiction, you need to master character, dialogue, narrative drive, point of view, intensity, and a hundred other things. Sometimes you get lucky and the first story flows out as if dictated by the Muse. If your luck holds, you get it published, and you think that's the way it's going to happen every time. Just in case it doesn't, here are some moves you can make to get the juices flowing again.

## Jump-start the Narrative Drive

Narrative drive is based on conflict and is the engine that drives your story. You have a character, the character wants something, and there are hurdles in the way. The story is about how your character deals with those hurdles. Narrative drive is the thing that grabs readers by the neck and pulls them along, reading page after page of your story, unable to put it down. It makes them want to hold on, keep reading, find out if the girl escapes from the gorilla.

One of my first writing teachers (a cute, redheaded guy fully worthy of the crush I had on him) said all stories are love stories—love for a girlfriend, a trombone, a motorcycle, a farm in Kansas. Good stories have characters, the characters want something, and they deal with a lot of stuff while they're trying to get it. The mother in the plane crash wants to get her kid out alive, but the exit is blocked by an injured nun. The guy in cubicle six wants to have an affair with the woman in cubicle four, but she's in love with the guy in cubicle five. The grandfather wants to leave his old Hudson to his grandson, but he's ill and running out of money and knows he could sell it to a vintage car dealer in town. Like it or not, you have to give up the idea of writing a sweet, non-conflict story. Every good story has at least two guys with guns.

To develop the narrative drive in your story, you must make conscious decisions about your characters—what they want and the hurdles that stand in their way. A few writers make these decisions instinctively, most don't. You need to get a solid grip on the conflicts to write a decent story. You may change or refine elements along the way, but you will waste a lot of time if you begin without them.

To start the narrative drive (see Figure 7):

- Draw a horizontal arrow from left to right with the tip of the arrow aiming to the right.

- On the left end of the arrow, write the name of your main character.

- At the tip, write one or many things she wants. Do this in one- or two-word phrases, just enough to remind you of the desire and not enough to clutter the page.

- Draw several vertical lines along the arrow. On each line, note a hurdle—one of the things your character has to deal with in order to get what she wants. The longer the story, the more hurdles you need. Two or three might do for a short story; a novel will require many more (see Figure 8).

In *Gone with the Wind*, Scarlett wants Ashley, Tara, and a comfortable life. Difficulties include Ashley's wife Melanie, the Civil War, the end of the plantation era, and Scarlett's relationship with Rhett Butler. The narrative drive, the thing

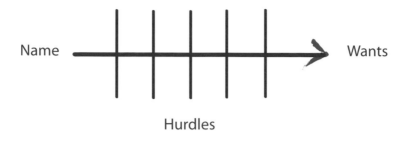

Figure 7. A Narrative Drive

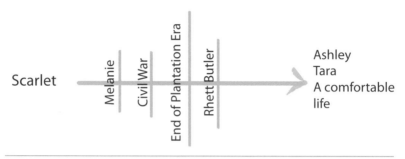

Figure 8. Narrative Drive for Scarlett O'Hara in *Gone with the Wind*

that carries a reader through the novel, is wondering if, how, and when Scarlett will get what she wants.

That's it! You can make it a whole lot more complicated if you want, but truthfully, this simple schematic is enough to jump-start the drive in your story.

Create one of these for each of the main characters in your story. Tape them to the wall near your computer, next to the Character Wheels you completed for your characters. The arrows will point the way and keep you on task. If you wander off the line—and you might—you will at least know you are off and can decide whether and when you want to get back on again.

## To Plot, or Not to Plot

I know many accomplished writers who don't believe in plots—they begin with a single idea or a line of dialogue and just start writing. They write like trains in a tunnel, seeing only what is immediately before them, easing through the darkness to the light at the other end. If this works for you—don't mess with it. If, on the other hand, you feel you could use a little boost, a bit more to go on, give "Bubbles" a try.

I'm referring to a Bubble Outline, a free-and-easy way to develop the skeleton of a story, the collection of bare bones that will eventually add up to a plot.

The Bubble Outline is not my invention. Many things in this book are, but this method is something I saw in a magazine article, and if I could find the author's name, I'd heap great praise upon her. It excited me when I saw it, and several years and adjustments later, I am still excited by the freedom and efficiency it offers. It has saved the sanity of many writers.

The process is quite simple. First, think really hard about the character and the narrative drive you created earlier. Your character wants something, and there are hurdles in the way of him getting it. What does he do to get what he wants? Does he go through a fire to get the girl? Where is the fire? Are other people in the scene? Does anyone get burned? As you imagine this scene, make notes about it in a circle (bubble). Then add another scene, and another, and another. After you have filled several bubbles with possible scenes, stare at them for a while, then decide which one you would like to write first, and second, and so on. Number all of the bubbles, and you have the beginnings of a plot.

That's the general idea. Now the specifics.

## Creating a Bubble Outline

Draw five, ten, or fifteen circles (bubbles) on a blank piece of paper. The circles should be just large enough to hold a few words (see Figure 9).

Now go back in your mind to the character and narrative drive you created earlier. Review just enough to get the feel of it again. Your character wants something, and there are hurdles in the way. As she struggles across the hurdles, things happen. Imagine specific events that might take place in your story. Focus on the people, place, and action—at *a particular moment*. Which characters are in this scene? Where are they? What's happening?

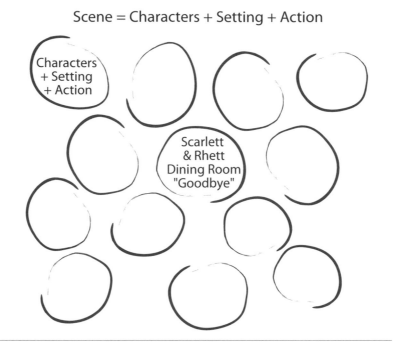

Scene = Characters + Setting + Action

Characters
+ Setting
+ Action

Scarlett
& Rhett
Dining Room
"Goodbye"

Figure 9.  A Bubble Outline

Near the end of *Gone with the Wind,* Scarlett decides she wants Rhett Butler after all. She returns to the house on Peachtree Street, finds him in the dining room, and confesses her love. Rhett isn't having any of it. In one of the most memorable of Hollywood scenes, he turns away with the famous line, "Frankly, my dear, I don't give a damn."

In subsequent chapters, we'll talk about how to write your scenes so they come alive. For now, just notice that you can capture an idea for a scene in very few words, just enough to trigger your memory when you are ready to write.

**Scene = Characters + Setting + Action**

Characters: Scarlett and Rhett

Setting: Dining Room

Action: Goodbye

Brainstorm as many scenes as you have bubbles, and add more bubbles if necessary. The best scenes are active, specific, and energetic. Sitting at the breakfast table watching the sun slant over the coffee cup is not active. Spinning the cup on a potter's wheel, is. Throwing the cup at the wall is. Throwing the cup at your sister really is!

Name the characters and the exact location. "Jeffrey" is not just "at home, fixing something," he's under the sink, stuffing rags up a pipe. The scene in the bubble would be: Jeffrey. Under sink. Stuffing rags.

Don't worry if some of your scenes are far-fetched; you can cut them later or add others. Also don't worry if they seem shallow; once you begin writing, you can dig deeper into the event and the psyche of your characters. For now, focus on the action—on where the characters are and what they're doing. The more specific your scenes, the more vivid they will be after you've written them.

## Put the Bubbles in Order

After the circles are filled, take a colored pencil or marker and number them in the order you think the scenes might appear in your story. Do this quickly, following your hunches. The numbering gives you a sense of direction— with flexibility. You have plenty of time to add, subtract, and recreate as you go along.

### Where Do You Begin Your Story?

There is always one scene that calls to you more than the rest, one that you think might be fun—or just more interesting—to write. Go with that instinct.

There are many possible beginnings, the worst of which is to tell readers everything you think they need to know to understand the situation. Expositional, fill-in-the-background openings are boring. Go for the meat, a scene that makes your heart pound. After that, you might want to tell us how your characters got to that point, or go along chronologically, or follow a drum beat of hard and soft scenes. Pick any sequence that seems right to you and number the scenes that way. This is your story, and you get to write it as you please.

### Writing the First Scene

Students in a Shut Up & Write! class started with a true event: a train derailment near a small town in Wisconsin. The wreck caused a chemical leak, and, according to news reports, all of the townspeople were evacuated.

The story got more interesting when my aunt, who lived nearby, said that she knew of one man who had not evacuated with everyone else, who was hiding out in his little house in town.

The class took those facts and made up the rest of the story.

They created a grumpy retiree named Alvin Harris and sketched a narrative drive (see Figure 10) in which Alvin's desire is to stay in his home and be left alone. His hurdles are: The chemical leak. Cops. The evacuation. His sisters coming after him. No food. No beer.

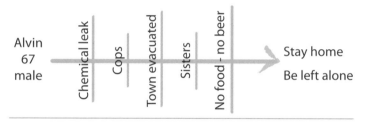

Figure 10. Narrative Drive for Alvin

With these thoughts in mind, the class brainstormed things they thought might have happened while Alvin was hiding out (see Figure 11). These were written on the board, in circles, in no particular order. Only after the board was full of possible scenes did the class go back and number the circles in an order that might work for the story. As usual, the numbering process felt haphazard while it was going on, but it shaped into a story quite quickly.

1.  Alvin and his friend Mike in the living room after the crash.
2.  Alvin at the liquor store, loading up.
3.  Alvin on the street, trying to hide from police helicopters.
4.  Alvin hiding in the bathroom while his sisters bang at his door, trying to get him out.

Figure 11. Bubble Outline for Alvin

5.   Alvin and his dog Rex steal food from the neighbor's house.

6.   Alvin and Rex pee on the neighbor's front lawn. (He never liked the neighbor anyway.)

7.   Big scene in the kitchen when the cops arrive to take Alvin away.

That evening Bert Kelley, one of the class participants, wrote the opening scene of "Alvin Harris's Cherished Quiet Time." He kindly agreed to let me use his writing as an example of how naturally you can write when you have the character, narrative drive, and first scene clearly in mind. If I gave Bert a chance, he would rewrite this, but I want you to see the freshness and energy sparked by this process.

> Alvin Harris sat in his Hoveround® in his living room full of World War II memorabilia and American flags, of Wheelchair Basketball trophies and marksmanship plaques, and grumbled at all the cowards who raced through town to get away from the derailed train and chemical spill. What the hell did they know about chemicals! His own government had gassed and poisoned him with Agent Orange, and did he cut and run? No, he stood his ground and let his rifle do the

talking. And did he get a hero's welcome home? Nobody even talked about it.

Now look at them run. Pathetic. He wheeled across the living room to his TV-watching spot and clicked on the tube, which clicked and flashed a light in the center, then faded out like a camera flash. Power was out. "Crap!"

He dropped the remote in his lap and looked through the archway into the dining room, where his dog sat. "Psssst! Rex! Paper!" said Alvin, and Rex, a sheepdog whose coat and beard were growing into what looked like moss for need of a bath, slunk his way to the living room with the morning paper, which was delivered through the mail slot every day.

"Good boy!" said Alvin, accepting the newspaper and turning to the horoscopes. He was absentmindedly petting Rex, reading not his horoscope but his high school sweetheart Julie Parker's, reading what the stars had in store for someone else, when a Galaxy crashed halfway through his window.

"Jesus Christ! Mike Patchel, where did you learn how to drive?"

Mike rolled down his window. "Awww shit. Goddammit!" He tried to push the door open, it only opened halfway, and he squeezed his way out and stood in the flowerbed. "Alvin, you okay?" shouted Mike through the hole in the wall.

"If you got insurance I am. Otherwise you're going to be fixing this and I'll be right here watching you!"

"I got insurance. Can't call the cops, though. They left town, too! What are you doing here? Let's get out of here, man, there's a chemical spill!"

"I'm not leaving for that. They don't even know if there was a spill for sure."

"Well, don't say I didn't warn you. I'll send the first cop I see back to do an accident report."

"Just go. Whatever," said Alvin, watching Mike trot across the yard. Alvin wheeled close to the screen door. "I know where you live, Mike Patchel! I know where you live!"

Alvin wheeled back over to the living room and surveyed the damage. The entire front end of the car sat exactly where the television used to be, and there was a hole the size of, well, a Galaxy 500 in his wall where the window had been. Glass and plaster and wood were everywhere. "Just my luck. Son of a bitch!"

## A Scene within a Story

In an earlier chapter, you met Dave Howard and Griffin, the main character in his novel *Griffin Peake.* Here's a draft of a scene Dave wrote about Griffin meeting the cat Lemuel.

As in the scene Bert Kelly wrote about Alvin, you see how just a few words written in a bubble (see Figure 12) can grow into pages of vivid writing. Notice how clearly you see what Griffin sees, and hear what he hears.

Figure 12.  Bubble Scene for Griffin

Griffin Peake woke from dreams of hot metal, fire, and smoke to the sound of crying. The sound was an uncanny wail, rising and falling slowly, muffled and oddly pitched. He sat up and looked toward the windows, three pale rectangles showing dimly at the far end of his attic bedroom. The crying was coming from there, outside.

The sound fell away into silence. He reached a lean arm to his bedside lamp. He lay there another minute, listening, wondering if he should go tell Aunt Mia about this. He didn't want to seem like a little kid, scared of the dark. She'd get all clingy, thinking he was freaking about his nightmares.

The cry came again: sad or hungry or in pain, he couldn't tell. He threw back the covers and padded barefoot down the cold hardwood floor toward the windows, picking his way around heaped t-shirts and torn jeans, stubbing a toe against his Army boots, stepping around CD cases and tangled earbud wires, kicking aside a crumpled fast food bag. He twitched the curtain aside cautiously. There, perched on the sill outside the center window, was a large black cat. The animal huddled close to the glass, hunched over, looking cold and miserable. It stared up at him and wailed.

Griffin reached for the latch and pushed open the diamond-paned casement. The cat, a huge burly tom, glided into the room and hopped onto the floor. It stretched itself, then licked out its matted fur. It was not, as he had thought at first, really black, but a brindled pattern of dark gray and brown that shifted as the cat moved.

The cat turned about on the floorboards and fixed its gaze on him, and he noticed with surprise that it had only one eye. One of its ears was torn mostly away, and scars scored its face. "Hey, dude. You've had it rough, huh?" He reached cautiously out to pet it, and the cat pushed its head against his hand, half-standing on its hind legs. The cat purred loudly and meowed at him. It was not one of those sweet little kitty-cat meows, but a harsh, guttural cawing that seemed to come from about halfway down the cat's body. Griffin chuckled. "You're a bruiser, aren't you?"

Griffin sat cross-legged on the floor, leaning over so that his long blonde dreadlocks fell around his face. He scratched the animal behind the ears. There was no collar on the cat, no tags, nothing. "You belong to anybody? You got any friends?" The cat cawed at him. "What am I going to call you, huh, buddy?" He picked it up and stroked its fur. "How about . . ." he looked in the cat's single green eye. "Lemuel." The name came to him suddenly. Was that some archangel's name, or some demonic prince he'd read about somewhere? Anyway, it fit.

## A One-Scene Story

In the early 1980s, short story writer and poet Raymond Carver was a Writer-in-Residence at the University of Wisconsin–Milwaukee. To tell the truth, I didn't know he was such a big deal when I signed up to study with him. I thought he was just another writer guy. That probably worked in my favor because with no awe-factor going on, I could focus on writing.

The following year, I studied with another author who assigned all sorts of high-school stuff that annoyed me. One assignment was to write a scene in the style of someone famous, so I wrote a teeny-bopper's parody of a Raymond Carver short story. Carver saw it in a campus literary magazine and was kind enough to compliment the writer.

The entire story happens in one scene. Life enters—you see some of the so-called "Carvers" past and future—but all the action is contained in one bubble (see Figure 13).

Figure 13.  Bubble Scene for the Carvers

I don't remember how it started. We were sitting at the kitchen table. The oven was on LOW. It was getting dark. He kept wiggling the ice in his glass, staring at it. He goes, "You never did like it, did you?"

I go, "What? What didn't I like?"

"My writing." He goes, "You never did like my writing."

I pour myself another drink. I need a lot to get through these things. I go, "Dammit, Ray, why do we have to go through this every time you finish a story? Why can't you just be happy about selling the stuff and leave me out of it?"

"Because you're my wife. That's why. You're my wife and you don't like my work." He leans back in his chair—almost tips it over—sprawls his long legs under the table.

"I like it. I like it." I go. "Listen, you're a great writer. You get right inside people. Right inside their empty parts. And you write in plain English everyone can understand. That's real good, Ray. Not every writer can do that."

He keeps wiggling his glass. "Well, then, what don't you like about it?"

I want to change the subject but I don't know how. I go, "What don't I like about what?"

He starts screaming. "About my writing, goddammit. What don't you like about my writing?"

"Jesus, Ray. Please, please. Let's not go through this again." He keeps egging me on. I go, "All right, goddammit. I hate your endings."

"So you hate my endings, huh?" He leans forward, squints at me.

"Why do you hate my endings?"

"You know why. Because you never finish things, that's why. You just quit when you want to quit."

"My endings are realistic. You just can't take realism, that's all."

"I take realism just fine. I take it every day living with you."

He goes, "What do you mean by that? What was that crack about?"

I push my glass into the center of the table and get up. "You. It's about you. You never finish anything."

He grabs me by the arm. "Wait a minute. What do you mean I never finish anything?"

I just look at him.

He puts his hand on my breast and squeezes it a little. He goes, "I finish some things, don't I?"

I just walk away.

"Go Gazebo" by Judy Bridges
*The Milwaukee Road Review*,
Issue 4, 1983

CHAPTER FIVE

# POINT OF VIEW (POV)
## Seeing Eye to Eye

The first horror film I remember seeing in the theatre was *Halloween*, and from the first scene when the kid puts on the mask and it is his POV, I was hooked.

—David Arquette, actor, director, screenwriter

IN THE LAST CHAPTER, YOU BRAINSTORMED SEVERAL SCENES and picked one that called to you, the one you want to write first. Before you begin writing, take a short detour to decide which point of view is best for you and your story.

When I talk about point of view, I don't mean it in the philosophical sense. This point of view (sometimes called POV) is not opinion, not what you or your character think ought to be happening in the story or in the world. Your story or article might present a philosophical point of view, but that's not what an editor refers to when she scribbles POV in the margin. This POV is a convention, part of the craft, a set of rules that make it easier for you to do the writing and easier for your reader to understand, and appreciate, what you've written.

You have options. You can write in first person, second person, third person limited, or third person omniscient. The important thing is to know the differences, and to make a deliberate choice. When you choose a point of view, you look at your scene through a particular pair of eyes. You see it more clearly and therefore write more clearly.

## It's All about the Narrator

The first thing you need to know about point of view is that it is based on the physical location of the narrator—it is the point from which the narrator sees what's happening. If the narrator is one of the characters, he sees the action through that character's eyes. If the narrator is looking over the shoulder of one of the characters, he sees the action from that location. If the narrator is in the sky, he sees the action from on high. The narrator can say only what he can see, hear, and know from the chosen place, that is, from his point of view.

Notice that we're talking about the narrator here, not the author. The author is the person who comes up with the ideas and pushes the pen. The author creates the characters and situations, or, in the case of informational writing, researches the material and decides how to present it. The author selects a narrator she thinks will best connect with readers. The "narrator" is the person readers "hear" telling the story—the sailor, grandmother, teacher, or cop who acts as a reporter, spinning the yarn in a way that will appeal.

Sometimes the author identifies the narrator, as Herman Melville did in the first line of *Moby Dick* when the sailor/narrator says, "Call me Ishmael." A children's picture book might be narrated by an imaginary four-year-old. A novel set in Japan might be narrated by an imaginary geisha.

The narrator sees the action and tells the story from his or her vantage point.

## First, Second, and Third

When you are ready to select a point of view, you have options:

First Person

Second Person

Third Person Limited

Third Person Omniscient

## First Person

A first person narrator uses "I" when telling the story. He's at ground level. He sees, hears, feels, tastes, and smells everything in the scene as he walks through the room or ascends the stairway. He can see how other characters react, but he can't be inside their heads. He does not know what they are thinking or what they did the night before.

If the first person narrator is a child, she sees everything from three feet off the ground. She sees the bottom of people's chins. She sees belt buckles more clearly than bald spots. If the person standing near her is nervous, she is more likely to notice toe tapping than a twitchy eyebrow.

The geisha would feel her feet inside her shoes, see the curve of the man's shoulder, and feel the silk. She would share the scene from her point of view—the smooth skin, the rustling silk.

### Advantage

First person narration is powerful. It brings us deeply into the character. It is the most immediate, most intense point of view, especially when combined with present tense, as in, "I can hear heavy breathing, but I'm afraid to turn around."

### Disadvantage

Because the first person narrator cannot see behind the barn or be in anyone else's mind, this POV can be limiting to use in longer stories.

### Examples

First Person, Singular: The narrator "shows" us the world as she sees it.

> Dank air rose up the steps from the darkness below. When I reached the bottom of the stairs, I ran my fingers over the rough cement block wall and found the light switch. Bare bulbs on long cords lit up rows and rows of the nuns' trunks, though there weren't as many as there had been. An exodus occurred in the last years, and I might soon be a part of it. The choice the ruling council had given me was therapy or leaving, and in any case I would no longer be the Mother Superior.
>
> —From "Almost Leaving" by Carol Wobig

First Person, Singular: The narrator can share what she could have reasonably learned from other sources.

> While I was sitting at my desk that afternoon, feeling good about how quickly I could do the math assignment, my mother tried to kill herself. She wandered out onto the road before the pills took effect, walked a few yards to the east, and collapsed in the tall grass. A neighbor on the way to town saw her and called an ambulance. Later that day, I pictured her lying there, perhaps parts of her body exposed, and was shamed to the core.
>
> —From "The Haircut" by Carol Wobig

First Person, Plural: The narrator speaks as "we" rather than "I."

> Late afternoon sunlight made long shadows prostrate themselves before us. We didn't notice. Warm breezes stirred our hair. We tossed our pigtails back impatiently. The chimes of the ice cream truck sounded on the next block. We didn't care. We had Lisa's new ball, Susan's new glove, and Tina's new bat, and possession of the diamond in Fielding Park.
>
> —Example written by Annie Chase

First Person, Present Tense: Adds intensity.

> I know what comes next. My taxi will wind through the scrubby brown hills of Los Cabos, each crest bringing me closer to the Sea of Cortez. We'll pass under an old stone archway, and just as it looks as though we could only go up, we'll turn sharply downward, straight for the coast where my hotel sits at its beachy feet. I know the arrangement of the sculptures in the rock garden behind it; I know the white wooden cross that sits on the peak of the hill to the north.
>
> —From "The Man Who Would Have Known Me" by Laurel Landis

## Second Person

Second person point of view is a little out of step with first and third since it has less to do with the position of the narrator and more to do with a form of address. The narrator refers to one of the characters in the story, or to the reader, as "you." "You were only six when you jumped off the cliff." Or, "You should have seen the way this klutz behaved."

## Advantage

Second person narration is useful for promotional and instructional writing, such as in this book where it seems natural to address the reader as "you."

## Disadvantage

Readers tend to rebel when they think they would not behave like the "you" in the story.

## Examples

The narrator refers to a character in the story as "you."

> Before you turned mean, it was easy. Even after you realized it was happening, you made it easy for us.
>
> —From "Jesus Did It First" by Annie Chase

Addressing the reader as "you" is often used in advertising.

> It's the perfect getaway for just the two of you. Melt into one of our sumptuous suites, each with a king-sized bed, custom mattress and Egyptian cotton linens.
>
> —A magazine advertisement for a hotel

## Third Person Limited

Third person limited point of view is almost as immediate and intense as first person. In this commonly used form, the narrator "rides with" one character in the story, seeing places and people from that person's point of view as if looking over his shoulder.

## Advantage

The narration feels comfortable and well anchored to readers.

## Disadvantage

None I can think of.

## Example

The narrator "sees" from Ronco's perspective.

> Outside, Ronco sat on the deteriorating wooden steps that hugged the back of the bakery building. He pulled the miniature bride from his pocket and ran his fingers along its plastic swells and dips. An oversized

dumpster hulked next to the building like some kind of animal absorbing the lingering warmth in the wall's bricks. The dumpster's lid was thrown back and the smell of the day's uncollected garbage assaulted him: soured milk, over-ripe produce, and other things he didn't want to imagine. It had been almost an hour since Jensen and the guys had stumbled down the alley, shrinking to the size of the small figure he held in his hand and disappearing into the crowds of customers moving from one Brady Street bar to another. He had been waiting under the light that filtered down from the transom above the back door this long. He could wait a little longer.

—From "The Guy in the White Socks" by Sara Rattan

## Third Person Omniscient (a.k.a. Unlimited)

The third person omniscient, or unlimited, narrator is up in the sky and godlike. She can see into every nook and cranny and inside every brain all over the world, all at once. She can even see what's going on behind the barn.

### Advantage

It is convenient to have such freedom and to be so wise.

### Disadvantage

Tempts the author to bounce from place to place and brain to brain, causing the reader to feel unhinged. Can also make the reader feel distant from the characters and action.

### Examples

When deftly written, omniscient narration is both panoramic and internal.

Directly overhead the sun blazes hot and bright against the vivid blue sky. Colorfully clad women work their hoes between rows of lush green tobacco plants. Grace Kangai pauses to catch her breath, squinting hard against the fierce noonday light. She works despite her weakening eyes. She doesn't need to see; years of experience have trained her hands to turn soil without harming the delicate roots of the plants.

"*Maiwe!*" Distressed, Gladys calls from several rows away. "*Mbuya*, Grandmother, why are you straining yourself in this hot sun? It will damage your eyes more! The rest of us can cultivate your rows when we finish ours."

Grace Kangai goes back to work. Despite what the others say, she refuses to believe her eyesight is failing. She calls back: "Who picks every pebble out of the mealie-meal to make the smoothest *sadza*?"

The women reply: "You, *Mbuya*! No one cracks a tooth eating porridge in your house."

"Who teaches the children to see weeds among young and tender tobacco shoots?"

"You, *Mbuya*! When you help them, the young ones never mistake crop for weeds."

Still hopeful she can convince Grace to rest, Gladys steps forward. "Young Boss is pleased with their work. But *Mbuya*, it is not a bad thing that wise old eyes grow dim. It is a thing to be expected."

Who, Grace wonders, stepping at last into the generous shade of an acacia tree, fingers easing the ache in her lower back, sees this land as it was before? Before the government measured and parceled and sold away the earth, giving Old Boss right and title to these thousands of hectares? Before he built Riverview Farm and produced sons to whom he gave the land? Before he called to those scattered off their own land, the land of their spirit elders, to return to work again, but for him?

You, *Mbuya*.

—From "What Shall We Do?" by Jeannée Sacken

Omniscient narration can be confusing when the author moves from one perspective to another too quickly.

David hated looking in the mirror. His teeth were stained, broken, and missing. Shelley knew he was self-conscious about his mouth. She thought he was the handsomest man in the world, because she knew what was in his heart. He knew she loved him but it made him angry to be so poor he couldn't get his teeth fixed. When he kissed her, he always aimed for her cheek. It made her ache for him the way he avoided applying for better jobs, the way he mumbled when he talked. He always laughed with his mouth closed.

—Example written by Annie Chase

# Tips for Handling Point of View

- Unless omniscient narration comes so naturally to you that you never err in its use, choose either first person or third person limited. Both have just enough restrictions to hold you tightly to the page; your prose stays taut and you don't go flying around and losing the reader.

- If your chosen point of view isn't working, go back to the beginning and try again from another point of view. Many stories have been saved, or taken to a new level of interest, by switching from third person to first, or first to third. Sometimes the only way to know for sure is to try it.

- You can use more than one point of view in a piece of writing if you handle it carefully. Make the switch from one point of view to another at a natural break in the story. A natural break is a point at which the reader expects a change, such as the beginning of a new chapter or after a four-line break—or "white space"—in the text. Be sure to identify the new narrator immediately.

## Example

The author makes a clear shift in the point of view at an anticipated break.

> With difficulty, Celac made the top of the gate, but as he swung his body over, he lost his one-handed grip and fell hard on his injured side. Dizzy from the pain, he forced himself to stand, to breathe. To go on.
>
> [Author inserts white space and immediately identifies the new point of view.]
>
> Stephen paused at the place where the man had fallen. There was blood on the concrete, more than he expected. Deciding it was time to take full measure of his opponent, as well as strengthen the bond between them, he tasted.
>
> —From *Nocturne* by Elaine Bergstrom

# The Difference between Point of View, Voice, and Tone

"Voice" and "tone" are often mentioned in conjunction with "point of view," but they are not the same.

- "Point of view" refers to the location of the narrator.

- "Voice" is the personality of the narrator.

- "Tone" is the mood of the piece.

## Point of View = The Location of the Narrator

Point of view is the physical placement of the narrator—his eyeball view of the characters' world, the place from which he interprets the action and shares it with the reader.

### Example

The narrator is well anchored in one location.

> I couldn't believe what I was watching. My mother talking to a perfect stranger about her love life with my dad, waving her perfumed wrist in front of his pinchy nostrils. Too grossed out for words, I made a big show of leaving the room but stayed close enough to the doorway to hear what came next.
>
> —From "Jewel Tea" by Kim Suhr

## Voice = The Personality of the Narrator

As the author, you instill your narrator with a personality that's appropriate to the piece—friendly, easy-going, down-home, aloof, imperious, intellectual, instructive, thoughtful, reflective. Each narrator has his own personality, his own voice. Cowboy. Beauty queen. Reporter. Intellectual. Little kid. Adventurer.

### Example

The narrator takes on a personality that suits the story.

> Meet Charles Goodfoote, Esq., PhD (Hon.), DD, JD, MD, Etc.
> Tracker of Man and Beasts, 1886: For those of you who don't frequent the press rooms of our large cities, and may not have read of

my exploits in the better sort of publications that are hawked on every street corner, I'll give a brief introduction to myself. I go by the common name of Charles Goodfoote. My original handle has been lost among the confusion of my early years, as I was raised by a band of Red Indians. My mother, poor woman, was a Blackfoot herbalist, married briefly to my father, an Irish muleskinner who died bleeding trade whiskey shortly after the rejoicing over my arrival slowed. I lived with my mother's people until the Army "rescued" me and shipped me off East to the Indian Barracks to unlearn my "Indianness," usually by the application of a cane across my nether parts.

My appearance in a glass would show hair like a raven's wing, a square jaw and a distinguished nose inherited from my maternal grandfather, the renowned Chief Stands-In-Thunder of the Peigan people. An erect carriage and above average height are part of the Indian package. A whimsical fate left me with one eye dark like my mother's and the other as blue as the sky, a condition respected among the Blackfoots, but a cause for consternation among the city folk I've consorted with over the years. From my father's side came a bushy handlebar mustache and a riotous temper, accompanying a keen wit and reflective view of life. In short, I'm a true son of the American West, with the heart of an Irish poet and the soul of a Red Indian.

—From *The Art and Science of Tracking Man and Beast* by Tom Hanratty

## Tone = The Mood of the Piece

Your story may be dark, light, sweet, romantic, witty, humorous, pensive, tense, dramatic, or sad. You and your narrator set the tone with choices of language, setting, action, and the sensual details you use. Every subtlety adds to tone, even the color of the water in the bathtub, even the sound of breathing.

### Example

The mood is so thick you want to help Theo pull away.

It was dark in there, the blinds down and drapes shut. Theo stood for a moment listening to his mother's slow breaths, then walked over and stood by the bed. She was lying on her front with her face turned to the side, mouth open and arms by her sides, hands open. Who slept like this in the middle of the afternoon? He reached out and touched her shoulder. Her skin was warm, and for a second he wanted to climb in next to her like he used to, and lose himself in the waves of her breathing. But he didn't. He was too old for that now. Instead he went back to his room and took apart his Lego Mission Commander, arranging the pieces in piles on his bed before beginning to rebuild.

—From "The Ghost Mother" by Felicity Librie

## Putting It All Together

When you write the first draft of a scene, you are too busy trying to visualize and get the words down to bother thinking about voice and tone.

He had to bend a little to see what she'd seen. Under the lowest branches of the pine trees, he could see a lush green rectangle of meadow beyond. Had he not known better, he'd have thought it was a great expanse of moss. He thought he heard her camera click.

When you rewrite, all of the elements—point of view, voice, and tone—start coming into focus.

He had to bend a little to see what she'd seen. In the distance, beneath the lower branches of the pine trees, the meadow formed a lush rectangle, as green and luminous as moss. He closed his eyes and saw the bear there, imagined Gwen's camera click.

—From "Olagam" by Laurel Landis

Study this one for a while. Notice that as the author tightens the point of view, we see the scene more clearly. She also identifies two other characters, the bear and Gwen, making the voice more intimate. Adding "luminous" to the moss and having the protagonist close his eyes make the tone of the scene a little mystical. The rewrite is actually four fewer words, but a big change.

# CHAPTER SIX

# SHOW AND TELL

The greatest thing a human soul ever does in this world is to see something and tell what it saw in a plain way. Hundreds of people can talk for one who can think, but thousands can think for one who can see. To see clearly is poetry, prophecy and religion, all in one.

—John Ruskin, critic, essayist

Don't say it was "delightful"; make us say "delightful" when we've read the description. You see, all those words (horrifying, wonderful, hideous, exquisite) are only like saying to your readers "Please will you do my job for me."

—C. S. Lewis, novelist

YOU'VE HEARD IT BEFORE: "SHOW, DON'T TELL." Sounds simple enough, but how do you know when you're "telling," and how do you write so it "shows"?

And what's the big deal about showing, anyway?

The big deal is that people remember the things you show. When you take a "tell" sentence like this, "His momma was mad at him," and turn it into a show-stopper like this: "Momma's eyes opened and changed from drunken and dreamy to angry, the eyebrows arching up and then down like terrible black wings," you know your reader will remember Momma.

Of course, you can't "show" all the time. If you wrote every line with that kind of energy, you would completely exhaust your readers. You need to "show" *and* "tell"—"show" what you want to show and "tell" what you want to tell. The trick is to know one from the other and be able to write each at will.

When you "tell," you transmit information.

When you "show," you knock your readers' socks off.

# A Side-by-Side Look at "Show" and "Tell"

### "Show" Writing

- Uses sensory detail
- Engages readers in the action
- Gives a sense of immediacy
- Makes readers feel

### "Tell" Writing

- Uses facts, figures, information
- Summarizes the action
- Covers long stretches of time
- Helps readers understand

**The Big Deal about "Showing"**

Readers feel as if they were there when it happened

**The Big Deal about "Telling"**

Readers feel as if they understand what happened.

**Examples of "Shows"**

Julio is a constant, comforting presence in my office. He leans back against my chest and watches what I type on the screen. He purrs at me and I don't want to move.

**Examples of "Tells"**

My cat likes to sit on my lap when I'm on the computer.

"Ooh, it's the birthday boy! Auntie Lena wants to give him a bi-ig kiss!" She clutched him, her fat fingers digging into his ribs, and he couldn't help it, his bladder let go as Lena's red lipstick-slick lips kissed him.

Aunt Lena always made Eddie uneasy because she had a habit of grabbing him and talking baby talk to him.

Lenny smoked one of his last three cigarettes and squinted as *The Jerry Springer Show* flickered in black and white, where a fat woman with no teeth had just torn off her shirt and was exposing her floppy breasts to the audience. Mercifully, the cameras had pixilated the image. On the faded wallpaper, a cockroach cleaned its antennae.

Lenny lived in a rooming house. There were cockroaches that lived there too. He seldom left his room, preferring to watch his black-and-white TV. Today, he was watching Jerry Springer. A woman showed her breasts to the audience, but Lenny couldn't see anything because the TV people had blurred the image.

Lenny and Auntie Lena no doubt have you feeling a little uneasy by now. Such is the power of good "show" writing. You can hear the cat purr and feel the fat fingers digging in your ribs.

"Show" writing is sensory, active, immediate, and deep. It makes you feel as if you are right there in the room with the characters. "Tell" writing gives you the same information but is not nearly as vivid.

## Use Your Senses

Your senses are your most powerful writing tools. It is through them that you perceive the world and translate your perceptions to your readers. You can talk about kittens all day and not make a dent, but if you can get your reader to see the white-tipped ears, hear the purr, feel the nubby paws, and smell the cat food, you have writing that's alive.

*Los Angeles Times* columnist Al Martinez wrote about a favorite teacher, Calla Monlux, who "saw something worthwhile in this sixth grader" (he says he was halfway to hell by then) and encouraged him to write.

> "You have a very special gift," she said, "and it can take you to a very nice future. But it needs nurturing." She sat me down after school and told me to close my eyes. Then she read me parts of a William Wordsworth poem: "I wandered lonely as a cloud/That floats on high o'er vales and hills,/When all at once I saw a crowd,/A host of golden daffodils;/beside the lake, beneath the tree, fluttering and dancing in the breeze."
>
> When she asked if I could see them, I said no. "Visualize," she insisted. "The sun is warm. The breeze touches you." She read the poem for me again and again, each time describing, each time demanding, each time transforming words into imagery.
>
> The daffodils emerged in a corner of my mind all buttery and golden, and the breeze touched my face with the warmth of a baby's kiss. My eyes still closed, I described what I saw and felt, and Miss Monlux, in a tone blending pride and knowledge, said, "You've learned the most important lesson you'll ever learn about writing. You've learned to visualize. Now put on paper what you see in your heart."
>
> —From "A Vision of Daffodils" by Al Martinez, *Modern Maturity* magazine

## An Exercise in Showing

Look at the list below. Pick a place that's familiar to you. Focus your attention on it. Use your senses to recall details and to bring the setting to life in your imagination. Write about it quickly and simply, as if you were writing a note to a childhood friend. Then read your writing to see what works.

**Pick one of the places on this list:**

| | | |
|---|---|---|
| Your bedroom | The zoo | A park |
| Back seat of a car | Garbage dump | A library |
| A schoolroom | Your friend's house | A kitchen |
| A ballpark | A barn | A church |

**Close your eyes and pretend you are in that place.** Really concentrate and use your imagination.

Who is there?

What are they doing?

How do things look, sound, feel, taste, and smell?

**Pick up your pen and write quickly.** Write without stopping or lifting your pen from the paper. Make no corrections in this first draft. Stop when you have filled a page or two.

**Read what you have written.** If you feel as if you are actually in that place again, you have written to "show."

### Example

In this piece of flash fiction, the author uses sensual detail to show the setting. The reader sees the gray patterns on the wall and feels the pale white sheets.

> I watch him put his clothes on. After he leaves, I feel numb. Another stranger takes off before midnight.
> I feel miniscule. Shades of gray, patterns on the wallpaper.
> Pale white sheets bury me in bed.
> I watch the lights of passing cars float by on the walls.
> The next day, I lie on the living room rug as they carry all the furniture off. It seems random, rather unpredictable. Did I live here?

The last thing they remove is the first thing I hung. It's my
empty birdcage.
I walk around the blank shell like a visitor.

—"Shades of Gray" by Robert Vaughan,
www.Amphibi.us

## Now, Take It Another Step

Settle into your writing space—your studio, a coffee shop, a spot on a park bench.
Have your notebook open and your pen at hand, but not *in* your hand. Take a
deep breath and imagine:

"Two guys get in an argument at a carnival."

That's it. That's all you need. Close your eyes and visualize the scene. Really
use your imagination. What do you see, hear, feel, taste, smell?

Now, open your eyes, pick up your pen, and write quickly. Fill a page or two.
When finished, ask yourself:

- How does "show" work in this piece?

- What specific actions tell you about the characters?

- What sensory data is included?

- How does it affect you as a reader?

- Do you care about the characters?

- Will you remember them?

If you are lucky enough to do the carnival exercise with a group and share
your results, you will notice that no two people write the same story, and each
person has a unique way of making you feel as if you are inside the scene. One
person shares a story of tattooed bikers threatening with hairy fists. Another has
a dad trying to reason with the jerk who grabbed the corn dog right out of his
daughter's greasy hands. In both cases, you feel the heat and smell the mustard.

## Example

Here is the carnival exercise Sara Rattan wrote in a Shut Up & Write class.

The Carny had to duck his head ~~when~~ each time he leaned ~~into~~ to give the safety bar a yank. ~~Dust. He was stil~~ And with each yank, the ~~three~~ tattoos ~~on his arm~~ on his upper arms <u>started</u>, like runners making a false ~~start~~ move before the starting gun fires. Still there seemed to ~~be He leaned back against the fence encircling the Tilt O Wirl's bright red saucers every time~~ Then, he ground the lever that brought a new ~~sauc~~ bright red saucer forward, one at a time, ~~This effort made the tattoos ripple~~ lurching and rolling crazily in smaller & smaller half moons until it came to a complete stop. It was a hot day and the lines were long, so ~~Marvin~~ Gordon had plenty of time to watch Evelyn watch the Carny as they ~~moved~~ crept up in line ~~closer~~. The closer they got to the tilt o Whirl, the softer the faded red tickets grew in the dampness of Gordon's ~~hand~~ clenched hand. ~~Why had he worn a polyster shirt. Feeling~~ He could feel dark wet circles spreading under his arms. Damn synthetics ~~conducted sweat like water conducted electricity. Why had he worn this shirt. He shrugged his shoul~~ shirts. Why had he worn it? He pulled at his collar, but the damp material clung stubbornly at his _____ line. He looked at Evelyn to see whether she'd noticed, but she was gazing at the Carny ~~like some insipid cow waiting for a trough to be filled.~~ "What -- " she said, startled by the weight of his look watching her. She pushed her hand right into his trouser pocket & found his fingers. That cooled him off, but just for a minute b/c they were at the front of the line & the Carny's voice oozed at them, made him flinch, like someone, too late, trying to avoid the spray of a puddle that a car's run through. "Hey, freshness. You ever bin on a Tilt-O-Whirl before? Watch your step." He had Evelyn's hand in his, pullin her up the hammered metal steps, she let go of Gordon's fingers. Her hand came right out of his pocket just like that. And just like that he felt the ~~stains under his~~ ~~wet~~ damp circles under his arms go completely wet. His face & forehead, too. He felt hot, sun-burned, all prickly & uncomfortable. And just like that he felt ~~the~~ his other hand, the hand with the soggy tickets come right out of his pocket ~~and come~~ and land on the Carny's upper arm. ~~The tickets flew loose in the air,~~

~~Showering the Carny's tattoos~~ He took out the tiger, then the ___lion___, then the _____American Eagle "What the hell, are you crazy man? He ~~ground the lever &~~ pushed Gordon off of

him & ground the lever, spinning Evelyn off, away from them both,
spinning crazily, around & around, on the Tilt O Whirl.

—Carnival writing exercise by Sara Rattan

Here are the opening paragraphs of the short story that evolved from Sara's carnival writing exercise.

The Carny ducked his head each time he leaned in to give the safety bar a yank. And with each yank, the tattoos on his upper arm started, like runners making a false move before the gun fires. He slapped the top of each car as he sent it off and then he ground the lever that brought a new bright red saucer forward, one at a time, lurching and rolling crazily—in smaller and smaller half moons—until it finally came to a rest.

It was almost noon. The crowd had begun to disperse to the Farm Bureau stands that lined the Midway. Some went in search of spit-roasted chicken and mashed potatoes served up by middle-aged women in hair nets. Others sought out corn dogs and fries at the 4-H Quonset, but it was the last day of the carnival's run and just as many clung to their place in line. Young girls hung on boys with bad skin. Army recruits, in tee-shirts meant to camouflage them, shifted their weight from side to side, watching the occasional exchange of chewed gum between the teenage couples. Fathers, unevenly anchored by a child on either side, pretended not to notice.

Gordon had plenty of time to watch Evelyn watch the Carny.

The closer they got to the Tilt O' Whirl, the softer the folded up strip of tickets grew in the dampness of Gordon's clenched hand. He could feel the dark, wet circles spreading under his arms. Damn Banlon shirt. Why had he worn it? He pulled at his collar, but the moist material stuck to his chest. He looked at Evelyn to see whether she had noticed, but she was gazing at the Carny—watching him slap the cars and grind the lever.

The tattooed leopard tensed and the tiger rose off its haunches, but the eagle didn't move. It was watching Gordon.

"Whyyy . . . Gordon." Evelyn was startled by the weight of his look. She pushed her hand right into his trouser pocket and found his fingers. That cooled him off, but just for a minute. They had come to the front of the line and the Carny's voice spattered all over him.

"Hey, Freshness, you ever been on a Tilt O' Whirl before? Watch your step." The Carny had Evelyn's hand in his, pulling her up the hammered metal steps and she let go of Gordon's fingers. Her hand came out of his pocket, just like that. And just like that he felt the damp circles under his arms go completely wet. His face and forehead, too. Beads of sweat stung his upper lip. He could taste the salt. He was broiling.

"This your old man? Got a couple of tickets for me fella'?"

Gordon didn't answer. He stared. The tiger fixed its eye on him.

And just like that, he felt the fist with the soggy tickets come right out of his pocket and land on the Carny's upper arm. He took out the tiger. Then the leopard. Then the American eagle.

"What the hell? Are you crazy, man?"

The Carny pushed Gordon off of him and ground the lever, sending Evelyn spinning off away from them both, sliding crazily, around and around, on the Tilt O' Whirl.

—From "The Carnival" by Sara Rattan

## Make "Showing" a Part of Your Life

Like Al Martinez, you have the opportunity to make showing a part of your life. This isn't something you do only when you are writing. You learn to pay attention more acutely, and do it all the time.

One of my favorite memories is of my dad driving a front-end loader around the yard. The bucket is lifted, and in it, my nephew Brian sits, proudly surveying the world. Dad lifts the bucket higher so Brian can touch the pine tree, the birdhouse, the top of my kid sisters' playhouse. Brian's job is to tell Grandpa what things are like "up there." Sharp needles. Rough bark. It smells like Christmas.

When I take young writers for a walk through the woods or an old cemetery, I stop them every few minutes and ask: What do you see? What do you hear? What do you feel? What do you taste? What do you smell? They taste flowers, sniff apple blossoms, and feel the smooth cold granite of a gravestone. This is ammunition for writing. This is a habit I hope they carry with them through their lives.

Whatever your age, you make your writing better, and your life richer, when you make "showing" a part of your everyday, walk-around life. Pretend Miss

Monlux is walking with you. She stops you every once in a while and reminds you to:

- Pay attention: Look closely. Notice the details.

- Use your senses: Stand still. See, hear, feel, taste, smell.

- Use your imagination: Daydream. Make up stories. Visualize.

- Practice writing: "Show" your characters, the setting, the action.

The sun is warm. The breeze touches you.

See the yellow daffodils.

And write what you see in your heart.

CHAPTER SEVEN

# WRITING FROM THE INSIDE

Maybe we're here only to say: house, bridge, well, gate, jug, olive-tree, window—at most, pillar, tower—but to say them, remember, oh! to say them in a way that the things themselves never dreamed of so intensely.

—Rainer Maria Rilke, poet

My grandfather was lame. Once they asked him to tell a story about his teacher. And he related how the holy Baal Shem used to hop and dance while he prayed. My grandfather rose as he spoke, and he was so swept away by his story that he himself began to hop and dance to show how the master had done. From that hour on he was cured of his lameness.

That's the way to tell a story!

—Martin Buber, philosopher

THIS IS WHERE YOU PUT IT ALL TOGETHER—your ideas, the characters and scenes you created, your decisions about point of view, and how you show what you see. It's all inside of you, waiting to come out. You have the skills, plus the story, plus a lifetime of memories, plus the passion to write. It is time to tap that well, to write from the inside.

When you write from the inside, you draw out your best natural qualities—empathy, imagination, love of language, a desire to communicate—and craft them into heartfelt paragraphs and pages.

The phrase "writing from the inside," has two meanings. You write from inside yourself and from inside the scene.

## Writing from Inside Yourself

The story you want to write is inside of you, not on the sheaf of papers you hold in your hand. The story on paper is only the current representation of the one you have inside. You could lose the paper version and still have the real one, the one that matters. It might take some time and trouble to reconstruct and you might forget parts of it, but it's still yours, still in your heart. All the stuff you collect over a lifetime, all the memories and research and bits of learning and imagination are yours to use. Add the plan for the current writing—the story idea, the article assignment—and you have everything you need inside you. All you need to do now is let it out.

## Writing from Inside the Scene

Rather than trying to write the whole story, begin with a specific scene—a particular moment in the story when something interesting is happening. Pick a scene that calls to you, scratches at you. Your scene might be one of the bubbles you brainstormed, or it might be one that's been twirling around in your mind, begging to be written.

**Example**

This is the opening scene of a story that won first place in the Wisconsin People & Ideas/Wisconsin Book Festival Annual Short Story Contest. In "Anything that Sticks," the author writes from inside the scene, sharing the experience of a fifth-grade boy who has Asperger's syndrome.

> Carter Conway presses the tip of his index finger against the point of his pencil. He lifts his desk lid to check his other pencils. "Fifth graders," he says sharply, like a teacher. "I hear chattering in this classroom. Too much chattering."
>
> Cutting through all of the babble, however, Carter also hears that someone is using the manual pencil sharpener. He likes the grinding sound the sharpener makes when the handle is turned, and the way the wheel can be adjusted to accommodate different-sized pencils. He also loves the smell of the shavings in the canister, and is always quick to volunteer to take them to the garbage pail so that he can watch the tan flakes that smell like his grandfather's workshop fall slowly into the can. The electric sharpener, he always says, makes the shavings too dusty, and they don't smell good. No thank you, he would rather not empty that canister.
>
> —From "Anything that Sticks" by Sheila Hanrahan,
> *Wisconsin People & Ideas*

# A Step-by-Step Guide to Writing from the Inside

The story is inside you. By following these steps, you can move the story from your mind onto the page:

1. Focus on a scene

2. Select a point of view

3. Position your adoring reader

4. Arrange your tools

5. "Walk" into the scene

6. Write the first draft quickly

## 1. Focus on a Scene

You can write only one scene at a time, so forget all the rest and focus on the one you want or need to write now. Draw a circle. Inside, jot down the three main elements of the scene: Characters + Setting + Action.

> Characters: Which characters are in the scene?
> Setting: Where, exactly, is this happening?
> Action: What is happening, right now?

For the scene "Two Guys Get in a Fight at a Carnival" (page 67), the circle contains:
> Two guys
> Carnival
> A fight

For the opening scene in "Anything that Sticks" (page 74), the circle contains:
> Carter Conway
> Classroom
> Fingering pencils

## 2. Select a Point of View

Remember that the point of view is the position of the narrator—the point from which the narrator tells the story. Attach yourself to a main character in the story or to an observer—a dog, child, girlfriend, or person in the crowd. (For a review of "point of view," see Chapter Five.) Select one:

First Person: "I"—Sees through eyes of one character.

    An excellent choice.

Second Person: "You"—Useful for marketing, otherwise awkward.

Third Person Limited: "He/She"—Rides with one character.

    An excellent choice.

Third Person Unlimited (Omniscient): "He/She"—The "eye in the sky."

    Sounds a lot easier than it is.

## 3. Position Your Adoring Reader

This is the cure for the teacher who didn't like you, the one you see scowling when you get it wrong, the one who still makes you too nervous to write. Look around your home or a garage sale or a toy shop for a truly accepting friend, such as my stuffed gorilla Alfred. Other writers have adopted rocks, ceramic gnomes, bits of birch bark. If it keeps you writing and doesn't censor what you say, it's the right thing for you. You'll find an editor or get a critique later. For now, let your heart be free.

## 4. Arrange Your Tools

Pen. Paper. Keyboard. Cup of coffee. Cowboy hat. Glasses. Box of chocolates. Whatever you need plus whatever makes you feel good. Several years ago I quit smoking and found I absolutely could not write without a haze between me and the screen. I had to burn smoky incense in order to get any work done.

Some writers prefer having a writing place that's all set for them; I prefer to move around—studio, coffee shop, living room, park bench. As I write this chapter, I'm at the home of an elderly aunt, sitting in a breezy gazebo watching a herd of chickadees swarm the feeder. To save myself the hassle of collecting what I might need or want when I'm working, I fill a basket with cell phone, water bottle, tissues, small bag of almonds, notebook and pen, and treats for the dog. If I didn't wear my glasses on a granny-string, I'd have a pair in the basket. The basket has a handle so I can grab-and-go. I use a daypack if I'm seriously hitting the trail. (I sometimes hike and scribble along the way.)

The point is to make things easy for yourself. Get the little things out of the way so you can focus on what you really want to do.

## 5. "Walk" into the Scene

### Use Your Imagination

Start visualizing the scene. Don't worry about research, grammar, rules, or getting published. For now, all of that is beside the point. Let yourself sink into your imagination, into your belly, into your memories.

### Close Your Eyes

Focus on your scene. If you are in a coffee shop and think someone might stare at you, smile to yourself and let them wonder what's up. The point is to close out the world and go to your place, to the scene you want to see.

### Picture the Scene

See the characters, setting, and action. Who's there? Where are they? What are they doing? Stay with it. Don't wonder what happened before or what might happen after—stay in the moment and imagine that it's happening right now. Give yourself a few seconds to get focused on it. Let it come to life.

### Take a Deep Breath

I know, it's starting to sound like yoga. It's not, but writing does call upon your ability to relax. Breathe. One, two, three deep breaths. Let the air slide all the way down to your toes. All the way in and all the way out, so far out you feel your belly crunch. Exhale through pursed lips so you have to push the air a little. A little resistance is good for the soul. Slowly. One . . . two . . . three. . . .

### Position the Narrator

Position yourself as the narrator; you are located either within one of the characters in your scene—looking out through that character's eyes—or you are looking over the shoulder of one of the characters, or you are looking down from your seat in the sky. Settle in so you can see the place, people, and action from your chosen point of view.

*Use Your Senses*

With your eyes closed, pay closer attention to the scene.

- What do you see?

- What do you hear?

- What do you feel?

- What do you taste?

- What do you smell?

Don't worry if you don't connect the first time you go through the list of senses. Go through it again, one sense at a time, until you become aware. Then just relax and go with whatever you have.

## 6. Write the First Draft Quickly

Write as fast as you can. Do not stop to think. Do not correct. If you are feeling stymied, just keep writing. The only thing you need to do is make words. It doesn't matter whether or not they are good words; just make words and do it as fast as you can.

Keep pressing forward until you have at least one page full of writing. Neatness does not count. Be sloppy. If you are using a pen, write big and wild. Turn the paper upside down if it makes you feel more creative. If you work on a computer and are an edit freak, close your eyes while you write. Or reset the font color to palest gray so you can hardly see the words. Or try writing with a pencil. For a while, I was lucky enough to have an assistant who could read my writing even when I couldn't. When my inner editor drove me nuts, I switched from computer to dull pencil and turned the scribbled mess over to her, and when she handed it back, it wasn't all that bad!

If you are writing by hand and the sight of the mess makes you nervous, cover it. Play whatever trick you must play on yourself to kill your inner editor and fill at least one page.

# A Field of Daffodils

When we "write from inside the scene" in a workshop, I always ask who did the worst writing and if they are willing to share. Several hands go up, "Me. I did the worst."

Of course, it's never the worst. There isn't any such thing as *worst* and *best* when you write like this. What there is—and this I guarantee—is amazement at how well everyone does at making readers feel the scene. When the readings are finished, I go back around the group asking people to recall something from each writer's work. It never fails that everyone remembers at least one thing from each of the writings—a bright color, a pungent odor, the warm wind in a field of daffodils.

## Examples

Put yourself in the place of this author as she imagines this scene of Mother Regina's office "from the inside" and shares it with you.

> Mother Regina stood at the window of her office, her head cocked just so to catch the last light of the setting sun on her chin. Using a tweezers and a hand mirror she had confiscated during a locker search in the novitiate, she plucked the whiskers poking out along the edge of her wimple. She hated herself for doing this, and would have made a novice scrub the steps to the chapel if she had caught her in such a vain activity.
> "Mother?"
> Regina buried her tools in the depths of her habit.
> "Yes?"
>
> —From "A, B or C" by Carol Wobig

This next example is the beginning of one of my favorite novels. *The Tiger Claw* is the World War II story of a Sufi Muslim secret agent searching for her beloved through occupied France. As you read, ask yourself: Who are the characters? What is the setting? What is the action? What is the point of view? What things will stay in your memory long after reading this scene?

Pforzheim, Germany
December 1943

December moved in, taking up residence with Noor in her cell, and freezing the radiator.

Cold coiled in the bowl of her pelvis, turning shiver to quake as she lay beneath her blanket on the cot. Above, snow drifted against glass and bars. Shreds of thoughts, speculations, obsessions . . . some glue still held her fragments together.

The door clanged down.

"Herr Vogel . . ."

The rest, in rapid German, was senseless.

Silly hope reared inside; she reined it in.

The guard placed something on the thick jutting tray, something invisible in the dingy half-light. Soup, probably. She didn't care.

She heard a clunk and a small swish.

Yes, she did.

Noor rolled onto her stomach, chained wrists before her, supported her weight on her elbows and knelt. Then shifted to extend the chain running between her wrists and ankles far enough for her to be seated. The clanking weight of the leg irons pulled her bare feet to the floor.

She slipped into prison clogs, shuffled across the cement floor.

—From *The Tiger Claw* by Shauna Singh Baldwin

The following is the lead of an award-winning magazine article about a clown who, beneath the make-up, was anything but funny. The writer opens with a scene written in third person limited and deftly switches the point of view when it's time to broaden the story.

Late morning, Aug. 24, 1991, a Saturday. Ron Schroeder sits before a mirror in the back room of the Ground Round Grill and Bar on Brown Deer Road. A light coating of baby oil glistens on his face as he scoops white greasepaint from a jar.

Carefully, expertly, Schroeder paints a wide, exaggerated smile around his mouth, stretching from chin to cheekbones. High on his forehead he paints two arching eyebrows. With a greasepaint crayon, he outlines the smile and eyebrows in red, and with eyelash glue affixes a red rubber nose to his real one. Then the final touch— a wig of dangling red curls and a cone-shaped hat on top.

Schroeder flashes a big, showy grin at the mirror, then steps into the Ground Round's dining room to greet an audience of jittery grade-schoolers, moms and dads. Silly the Clown comes to life.

Meanwhile, across town at the Briarwick Pool Apartments in Greenfield, Schroeder's wife Christine is in a panic. Something is not right with the couple's 7-week-old daughter, Catie. She won't eat or sleep and doesn't respond to her mom's voice. The child stares blankly, her eyes not tracing as her mother's hand passes before her.

Christine Schroeder wants to take her daughter to the hospital: she has full medical coverage. But Ron had told her no. The baby just had a cold or flu and would be fine.

Christine abides by Ron's order. She's used to his iron-fisted control. And his anger. Soon after they began living together, he began to call her fat and ugly, she later told police. She dropped to 95 pounds. He would punch her on the side of the head and kick her in the legs, places where bruises wouldn't be noticed. And one day, when she was seven months pregnant with Catie, he flew into a rage, attacking her, dragging her into the living room and throwing her onto a couch.

Now she was just too afraid to cross him.

—From "The Joker" by Kurt Chandler, *Milwaukee Magazine*

In the following example, a guidebook description of a hike at Horseshoe Harbor in Upper Michigan, the author takes us to the shoreline. He makes us feel the wind before he moves on to the trail.

A certain aura, a whiff of raw fury, hangs on the shoreline here. Even on a benign summer day, the stark reefs of eroded conglomerate rock seem to speak of the epic storms of November; wind and waves sending spray sky high, and a timeless clash between the lake and the ancient bedrock.

—From *Hiking Michigan's Upper Peninsula* by Eric Hansen

# CHAPTER EIGHT

# NONFICTION AND THE ORGANIZED MIND

What separates the professional article writer from the novice—the selling writer from the unpublished—is what goes on that blank page. The pro attacks the paper with a plan that leads, step by steady step, from raw idea to a finished article.

—Editor's note in November 1993 issue of *Writer's Digest* magazine

First have something to say, second, say it, third, stop when you have said it, and finally, give it an accurate title.

—John Shaw Billings, nonfiction writer

Contrary to general belief, writing isn't something that only "writers" do: writing is a basic skill for getting through life. Writing isn't a special language that belongs to English teachers and a few other sensitive souls who have a "gift for words." Writing is thinking on paper. Anyone who thinks clearly should be able to write clearly—about any subject at all.

—William Zinsser, journalist, nonfiction writer

REGARDLESS OF OUR DAYDREAMS ABOUT SPENDING HOURS IN AN ATTIC STUDIO writing prize-winning novels, many of us spend hours every week writing nonfiction—articles, reports, letters, how-to manuals, and fact-based books about people and places.

People who write nonfiction often apologize, as if they are involved in writing of a lesser form. And yet we all know that a well-written essay can change a life as deeply as a novel. A best-selling book on business leadership changes corporate cultures for years. Each form, from leather-bound book to folded note, has its power. When a national magazine asked teens about their favorite writing, one girl responded that she loves the notes her mom puts in her lunchbox: "I'm so proud of you!" and "You're a great kid!" That's writing of a shorter form, but it's certainly not lesser.

One well-chosen line is enough for a lunchbox note. To write a two thousand-word magazine article, you might interview four or five people, collect facts and figures from several sources, and fill a couple of small notebooks. Then you have to go through it all and decide what to include, where to begin, where to end. All this happens *before* you start the actual writing. No one except a writer realizes how hard it is.

An article I wrote included some comments by a local business owner and was published with a nice, full-page photo of her. After the article's publication, a double-sided picture frame appeared on her desk. On the left side: the magazine page with her photo. On the right side: a letter of congratulations from the mayor.

I did not get a letter congratulating me for having written the article.

When you write stories, plays, humor, or poetry, you get recognition. When you write articles, nonfiction books, and business communications, you get paid. When you write both—which is what most of us do—you have an interesting life.

## The "O" Word

Intelligent, curious, resourceful writers rarely suffer a lack of information. Give us a topic and within a day we have more facts at hand than we know what to do with. Give us a week for an article or a year for a book, and we'll come up with five times the detail needed to fill the thing. If we don't know the right people to interview, we email our writer friends and ask: "Who do you know . . . ?" We get the facts, we double-check, we pile up bits of information and ideas about how to proceed. Then, when it's time to write, we go a little nuts. We know too much. We need to get organized.

While there is disagreement over whether or not story writers need to organize their thoughts before they begin writing, there is no argument about the need for organization when you work with information. In *How to Write Fast (While Writing Well)*, David Fryxell calls it "The 'O' Word."

The O Word—Organization—is the other face of the coin of discipline. Like discipline, it affects every aspect of a successful writer's work: How you organize your time. How you organize your workspace and your notes. How you organize your work itself, both in the simple sense of putting point B after point A, and in the deeper sense of the thematic structure of your work.

No way around it, you need to find a way to keep your thoughts and material under control, to get the big picture as you brainstorm and plan, to focus on one section at a time as you research and write. Organization speeds the process and makes the writing easier. It also helps your reader understand the material you present.

## The Big "O" for Creative Types

I'm not keen on dividing people into categories of left or right brain, creative or analytical, writer or engineer. I'm creative as all get out, yet every aptitude test I took as a kid said, "You'd make a good engineer." Engineers are creative. Writers are analytical. The trick is to use both sides of the brain.

The Alligator Outline is an organizational tool that blends both sides of the brain. It is similar to a mind map, cluster, or Ishikawa diagram, but with a sense of direction and lots of room for creative thought.

I invented the "Alligator" when I worked on a project for Winnebago Motor Homes and got myself stuck in a swamp of too-much-information. The business plan called for me to tour the manufacturing plant in Forest City, Iowa, then fly to several dealerships for interviews, then write the script for a twelve-minute video to be shown to potential customers. As we walked through the plant and came upon a nearly finished motor home, I said, "I really ought to make the trip in one of those!" and three hours later I was driving down the highway in a thirty-seven-foot, top-of-the-line Winnebago that had a queen-sized bed, full bath, and more kitchen appliances than I had at home at the time. The first stop was Louisville, Kentucky, where I attended the mother of all RV shows (imagine, a motor home with a hot tub and bar!) and learned that making a left turn with a thirty-seven-foot vehicle can be hazardous to the little car on your right.

After Louisville, I drove north to Canada (ice!), then zigzagged south through the Appalachians, down the East Coast, and on to the Gulf of Mexico. Along the way, I visited dealers, interviewed sales people, parked in campgrounds, and asked RVers, "Would you buy one of these? Why? If not, why not?" I read every manual and used every do-dad in the unit.

By the time I got to Florida, I was too well informed. I sat on the floor—notes, user manuals, and interviews piled around me—and thought, a twelve-minute video? How about a book?

I tried every organizational tool I knew—lists, mind maps, outlines—and finally came up with a sloppy mess that looked like a many-legged alligator. It was ugly, but it worked! I got the important stuff in the script, in the right order, and the client thought I walked on water.

Since then, I've taught this system to hundreds of people who use it to organize articles, books, proposals, reports, speeches, white papers, brochures, web content, and business plans. A few people use it for fiction, but I think Bubble Outlines work better for that.

## Alligator Outline

Think of the skeleton of an alligator, with a pointy head and a long, skinny line for the back and tail. Draw that on a piece of paper or a good-sized whiteboard. Draw the head as the point of an arrow, aimed to the right. That's where you put notes about your readers. The long spine of the alligator is where you put your message. At the far left—the tip of the tail—you make note of the voice you want to use. Making clear decisions about these basics—reader, message, and voice—gets you started in the right direction (see Figure 14).

Figure 14.  An Alligator Outline

## Step 1. Define Your Readers

At the head of the alligator, write short notes defining your audience. You can't write to "everyone." You almost never write to an infant or a person with severe dementia. You write to people who need or want this information, or who are likely to read the print or online publication in which your work appears. You write to persons of a certain age, lifestyle, education level, need, interest. What you want is to get a picture of these readers in your mind. Imagine what interests them and how best to approach them. Make your notes in one- or two-word phrases, rather than full sentences. Long notes just get you tangled in the language.

If you are writing for a magazine, look at the ads and articles—are they targeting adults? Kids? People who love dogs? Those are your readers. You need to see the world from their point of view.

At the head of the alligator for this book, I list my readers as: Smart. Creative. Practical. Adults. Interested in writing.

At the head of the alligator for the Winnebago script, I wrote: Seniors. Sociable. Financially able (see Figure 15).

Seniors
Sociable
$$ able

Figure 15. Alligator Outline: Audience

## Step 2. Focus Your Message

What, exactly, do you want your readers to understand? If you could get just one message across to them, what would it be? Coming up with the main point is one of the hardest parts of informational writing, but when you distill your thoughts this way, you are a long way toward accomplishing your goal.

## Sample Messages

| Project | Message |
|---|---|
| Magazine feature story | When you volunteer, you get more than you give |
| Personal profile | Louise O'Brien was the best ballroom dance teacher in town |
| Investigative piece | You could get hurt if you mess with these people |
| Round-up article or book | Twenty-four terrific places to take your kids |
| Thesis or report | Students at Downer High excel in sciences because . . . |
| Advertisement | This chipper-shredder does the job for you |
| Fundraiser | Hungry children need your help |
| Social change | Has sustainable agriculture come of age? |
| Personal essay | Why I wrote my own obituary |

Notice that several of the sample messages are addressed to "you," the reader. Phrasing your message that way makes it easier to get and stay focused on the reader.

Write the message along the spine of the alligator.

The message on the alligator for this chapter would be, "Here's a good way to get your thoughts organized."

The message on the alligator for the Winnebago script was, "You will enjoy owning this RV" (see Figure 16).

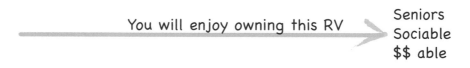

Figure 16. Alligator Outline: Message

If you hang your Alligator Outline on the wall near your work space, every look at it will remind you of what you want to say, to whom.

## Step 3. Decide on a Voice

This always reminds me of the caterpillar in *Alice in Wonderland*. "Whooo ahrrrr youuu?" Sure, you're Alice, the writer, but that doesn't mean you always use your own voice when writing. Depending on the publication and the audience and the point you're trying to make, you might choose one of several voices—the reporter for a newspaper article, the expert for a how-to book, the concerned citizen for a letter to the editor, the CEO for a book for business leaders.

Make a conscious decision about the voice you want to use and write that to the left, on the tail of the alligator (see Figure 17).

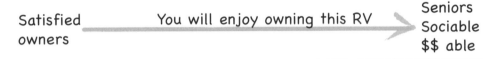

Figure 17. Alligator Outline: Voice

### Sample Voices

| Publication and Topic | The Voice You Might Choose |
| --- | --- |
| Book for business leaders | CEO of a successful company |
| Newspaper article about local politics | Reporter, either freelance or staff |
| Magazine article about women in prison | Reporter/attorney/prisoner |
| Profile of author in a writing magazine | Reporter/friend/another writer |
| Essay about city in a city magazine | Reporter/city resident |
| Fundraising letter | Friend of the cause/fellow citizen |
| Marketing piece | Satisfied customer |
| How-to book | Expert in field |

For the Winnebago script, I used the "voice" of satisfied owners, a married couple similar to those we thought would be interested in buying the product. The director hired actors who looked and sounded exactly as I hoped, except that they smiled too much.

## Step 4. Brainstorm Main Points

Now that you have the body of your alligator—your audience, message, and voice—you can start brainstorming the main points for your message (see Figure 18).

Draw several lines (legs) extending out from the spine of the alligator. Each leg is a main point. Don't worry about the number of legs; you can add and subtract later.

Brainstorm possible main points and note them—again in single words or short phrases—on the legs.

For the Winnebago project, you might have: Fun. Ease. Comfort. Safety. Service. Money.

## Step 5. Brainstorm Supporting Points

On each leg (point/category) of the alligator, draw several lines to accommodate the facts and figures that make the case for that leg's point. These lines should be at angles, attached to the legs. Your alligator will look like it has several legs, each with several feet or claws up and down the length of each leg.

The "claws" (supporting points) attached to the Winnebago leg labeled "Fun" are: travel. national parks. Arizona. grandkids (see Figure 19).

The supporting points attached to the leg labeled "Comfort" are: seats. suspension. bed. shower. storage. A/C. heat. carpet.

Sift through your research, interviews, anecdotes, facts, and figures. Add as many points as you want. If the alligator is getting messy, you're on the right track.

## Step 6. Brainstorm Sub-points

When you come across miscellaneous bits of information that you want to keep track of, write them on short lines attached to appropriate supporting points (see Figure 20).

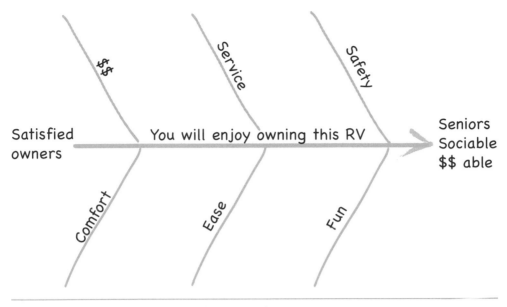

Figure 18.  Alligator Outline: Main Points

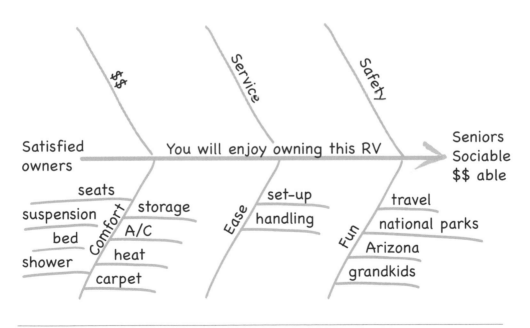

Figure 19.  Alligator Outline: Supporting Points

On the point, "Fun," we have the supporting point, grandkids, and on that the sub-point, Disneyland. Disneyland might turn out to be a throw-away, or it might be the perfect anecdote to illustrate a main point. You make that decision in the next steps.

### Step 7. Sequence the Points

Number your points in the order you think you might want to cover them. Pick one you think might work well as a lead or "hook" and label it #1 (see Figure 21). Don't worry if you are unsure—there's a good chance that your first take-a-flyer guess is the right one. If not, that's why you have an eraser.

My personal favorite is to start in the middle of a scene that illustrates my main point. For the essay about the elderly struggling to stay out of nursing homes, I selected a scene that illustrated one woman's physical loss in a very poignant way. You might have chosen another place to begin.

My least favorite lead is a definition, the one that tells the reader what the dictionary says, just in case she didn't know. Questions work. So do anecdotes. Quotation leads work, too, but can get tiresome because they're done so often.

Sequence all the points so that when you begin writing, you know what comes next. Indecision can keep you going in circles and writing about the first point over and over again for several pages, but if you have a sequence of points and sub-points, you'll automatically move from one to the next. If you decide on a full-circle piece, in which you end by referencing the beginning, your first and last numbers will be at the same point on the outline (see Figure 21).

Once you have numbered all of the points on your Alligator Outline, put a bold star next to the last one. You do this so it stays in the back of your mind while you're writing. When you have your ending in mind, your instinct will take you there.

## Tips for Using the Alligator Outline

- Work with a pencil on paper, or a dry erase marker on a whiteboard—things you can change or erase. Some people use computers, but it's hard

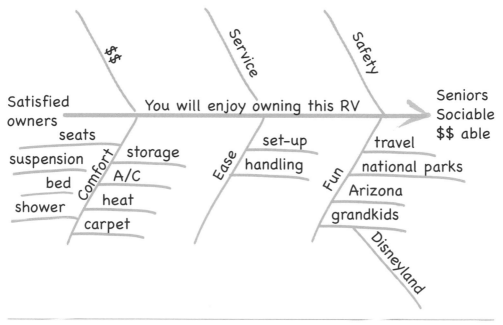

Figure 20. Alligator Outline: Sub-Points

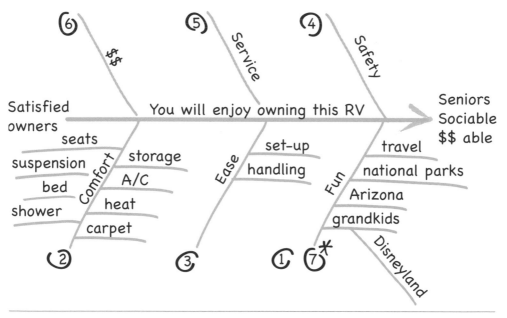

Figure 21. Alligator Outline: Points Sequenced

to change your mind about lines that look so pretty. Better to be sloppy, make mistakes, slap it on the wall, and see what sticks.

- Make each of your notes as short as possible. A sentence is too long. A phrase is almost too long. One word is best. "Safety" is enough to remind you to check accident statistics.

- Make research notes. If you need to check facts or do added research related to points you expect to cover, circle or put a check mark near the point. Use color if that helps—a green check for library, blue for Internet, yellow for interview, purple for notes you stashed in the purple box.

- If you need to do a lot of research, copy your alligator onto a sheet of paper that's portable enough for you to carry around with you. When you get to the library and unfurl it, you will see your notations and be more efficient with your work.

- Note sources near the points so you will have them for further research and to prepare a source list.

- Highlight related anecdotes. If you have a mini-story that helps to substantiate a point, insert a key word that reminds you of the anecdote. For instance, near "Disneyland," you might have the note "triplets," which will remind you of the grandparents who took triplets to Disneyland and lived to tell about it.

- Connect related thoughts with dotted lines.

- To get a rough idea of how much space you can spend on each point, divide the number of words the publisher expects by the number of points you want to cover.

- Cross out things that seem redundant or that you just can't fit into the space allowed.

- When you are ready to sort your collection of notes and interviews, write your main alligator points (1, 2, 3) on individual sheets of paper, tape the sheets to the wall or over a table, and go through your research, dealing it out into piles below the appropriate numbers. Print the notes you took on your computer (on used paper, of course), cut them so there's only one point per piece of paper, and sort them into the piles. When it's time to start writing on a particular point, you can pick up that pile and re-sort it according to your supporting points.

- When it's time to begin writing, take only one pile of material to your desk. This will keep you focused on one subject at a time. The rest of the stuff is there, waiting for you. You don't need to worry about it now.

### Sample Alligator Outlines

- Figure 22 shows university student Katie Lance creating an Alligator Outline to organize her senior paper.

- Figure 23 shows the Alligator Outline I used to organize facts and family stories to write a eulogy for my husband's grandmother.

- Figure 24 shows the finished eulogy as shared at Grandma Schroeder's memorial service.

## To Use the Alligator Outline for a Non-writing Project

Every month I get at least one call from a student who has used the alligator in a new and interesting way: to repair a motorcycle, to reorganize a bank division, to remodel a house, to plan a new career. It's as handy for organizing projects as it is for planning writing assignments.

To use the Alligator Outline to plan a project of any type:
- Write the goal at the head of the alligator, where you would normally put the audience.

- Write the various parts of the project on the alligator legs and claws.

- Number the parts of the project in an order you can follow to get things done.

Figure 22.  Alligator Outline: Katie Lance Organizes Her Senior Paper

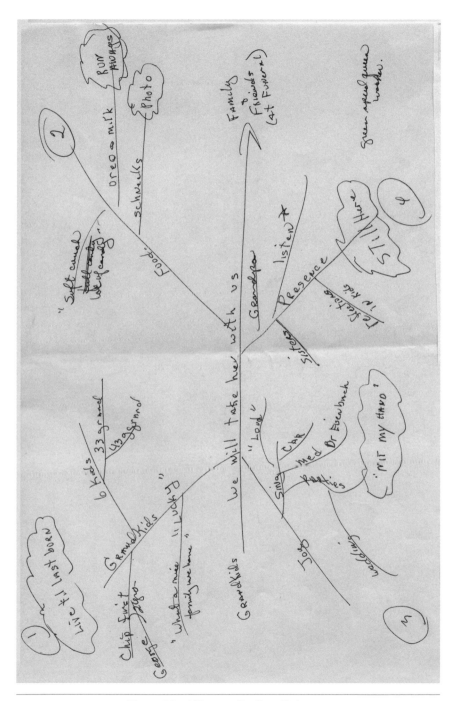

Figure 23.  Alligator Outline: Eulogy

### ...We Will Take Her With Us...

My name is David Blank. I am one of Anastasia Schroeder's many grandchildren, and today I'm going to try to speak for all of us. I don't for a minute think I can summarize all of our feelings. We each had our own, special relationship with Grandma Schroeder.

We weren't the only ones to have special relationships with Grandma. As I look around, I see people who knew her better than we did – her sisters, especially. They knew her when she was a little girl. They have stories and memories we can only guess at. Her friends have other memories; her children, still others.

We remember Christmases, rosaries, hats, baby caps and afgans. We remember that, at family gatherings, she would often look around and say, "How lucky we are to have such a nice family." Now, I'm sure there were days when she didn't think each and every one of us was all that nice. I could tell, for instance, that she didn't think I was so nice the day I ate half a plate of schnecks she'd meant for the whole family. She told me to *stop that*, in that voice that meant business – you know the one I mean.

Grandma Schroeder wanted to live until her last grandchild was born. She did. 6 children. 33 grandchildren – counting Marky and Antoinette, who have been with Grandpa, waiting for her. She also had 43 great-grandchildren. Enough kids and grandkids and great-grand-kids to make a party. A party with lots of singing.

Listen closely when we're singing, and you'll notice that it is Grandma's voice you hear. It is Ann, singing to her children, who sang to us, who taught us the songs we teach the next generation. She spooned medicine into tiny mouths to the tune of "Dr. Eisenbach." She sang "You are my Sunshine," "Good Night, Irene," "Johnny Ver Beck," and "Der Hoot." We sang with her and she would say, "Well, we don't sing good, but we sing loud!"

We each had our favorite songs. Mine was "Mit Mine Hand..." Do you remember that one?

1
Mit mine hand on mine self
vaht is das here
das is mine brain boxer me mahn de meer
brain boxer
brain boxer
ink-ee-dink-ee-do
das voht ve learn in da school

2
Mit mine hand on mine self
vaht is das here
das is mine eye blinker me mahn de meer
eye blinker
brain boxer
ink-ee-dink-ee-do
das voht ve learn in da school

3
Mit mine hand on mine self
vaht is das here
das is mine nose blower me mahn de meer
nose blower
eye blinker
brain boxer
ink-ee-dink-ee-do
das voht ve learn in da school

4-5-6-7
(add each of the following,
repeating the sequence as above)
food chopper...bread basket...
knee bender...foot walker

Grandma Schroeder knew how to have fun.

And she knew how to make a kid feel good. She had the world's softest couch and a candy dish full of M&Ms. When grandkids would visit, she'd pour milk, open a package of Oreos, and listen carefully to what we had to say. Our thoughts, our stories, our concerns, were important to her. Knowing that, made each of us feel important.

More than one of us followed the time-honored tradition of escaping from home and running away to Grandma's house. She'd pour the milk and pass the cookies and listen to us. When we were finished talking, she would say, "You can go home now."

It is Grandma who has gone home now. She is where she wanted to be – with Grandpa, in a softer, sweeter place.

But she is also here, with us. If you look around, you can see her in the way a grandchild smiles, or in the way a great-grandchild leans forward on her mother's lap and listens, just as intently as Grandma used to.

We are the reflection of the life she lived. Wherever we go, whatever we do, we will always take her with us. You will always be able to hear the echo of her voice in the songs we sing.

And we won't mind at all if you say, like Grandma did, "We don't sing good, but we sing loud!"

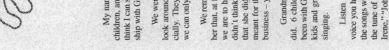

Figure 24.  Eulogy for Grandma Schroeder (written from an Alligator Outline)

# Chapter Nine

# CRITIQUES
# AND WRITERS' GROUPS

I never found out the moon didn't come up in the west until I was a writer and Herschel Brickell, the literary critic, told me after I misplaced it in a story. He said valuable words to me about my new profession: "Always be sure you get the moon in the right part of the sky."

—Eudora Welty, novelist, short story writer

The great critic is an artist as well. He tells us what he thinks is good, he tells us why he thinks so, and he performs both functions in such a way that we are excited by his manner while convinced by his argument.

—Winton Dean, critic

You mustn't fall into the trap of assuming that because nobody likes what you have done it is very good. Sometimes people don't like what you've done because it is terrible.

—Edward Albee, playwright

THIS CHAPTER IS ABOUT MAKING YOUR GOOD WRITING BETTER. It's about taking your manuscript and going public, showing it to people, asking for critiques and opinions, acknowledging that this version is as good as you've got "so far."

One of the joys of my life is being able to attend a writers' group that feeds my soul and sees my mistakes. Every page of this manuscript was critiqued at least eight times. The first read was mine. Second, my husband. Third, my critique group. Fourth, a hand-picked group of insightful writing friends. Fifth, a cycle of editor-publisher-editor-publisher (this went on for a while), and then me and my husband, again. Every time it was read, it was improved, usually quite a bit. The majority of the changes were made in response to comments made by my critique group, the finest group of writing friends a girl could have. Most of them attended one or another of my writing classes so they knew what I was talking about and whether or not I got the point across. If I did, they were happy for me. If I did not, they knew how to help. That's what you want from your writer's group.

The longer you write, the more you appreciate the value of critique. In the beginning, it's all about inspiration. Words fall out of the sky and all you have to do is write them down. Each piece of writing is perfect. Later, after you paper the bathroom walls with rejection slips, you take a cold, hard look at the pages and start to wonder.

Let's say that for the past year, you've been hunched over a desk, working on your magnum opus. The Muse visits from time to time and lights a candle, but doesn't stay nearly long enough. You like some of what you've written; other things, well, no matter what you thought at first and what your best friend says, you know they could be better. Maybe it's time to swallow the pencil and look for a critique group.

## Why Join a Critique Group?

You join a group because as wonderful as best friends are, they are not enough. You need a team of readers who are serious about the craft and have your interests at heart. The members help you see the wobbly point of view, the shift in character, the wrong label on a bottle of wine. They also point out the good things: the brilliant phrase, the perfect dialogue, the evil character you wrote so well you made the reader's skin crawl.

A good writers' group helps you stay on task. Members let you get away with not writing once in a while, like when you break your wrist or drop your computer in the lake, but if you show up too often with nothing, they will start looking at you funny. This is good peer pressure, the kind that kicks you in the butt on Friday so you have something to take in with you on Tuesday. Your Tuesday pages may be warm from the printer, but you will have them.

Another benefit of a group is that other writers are full of good advice. What you learned in school or even in a recent workshop is often old news. The industry shifts quickly, and staying on top of it is a full-time job few writers want or can handle. In a group, one person will be savvy about this, another about that, and collectively you make sense of the puzzle. Writers in healthy groups are happy to share what they know.

And best of all, a writers' group is a good place to make lasting friends. Not long ago, a member of my group injured her knee so badly that she needed to use crutches. Her basement flooded, she went down the stairs on the crutches, and, you guessed it, catapulted down the last several steps. Broken shoulder. Surgery. A lengthy recuperation. Her siblings were there to help, also neighbors and her friends from our writing group. They not only visited, brought food, taxied her to doctors' appointments, emailed, and called, they kept her writing light burning as well. They awaited the next of her stories and cheered her on. She, like others who love to write, has something to give the world, and her fellow writers didn't let her forget it. They would have printed and submitted her work if that's what she'd needed.

## How to Find the Right Writers' Group

Groups are as varied as the writers who join them, and finding the right one can take some time. Coffee shop flyers, online listings, and writers' publications all contain information about local groups. You might have to visit several. When you're shopping, ask yourself these questions:

### Does the Structure Work for You?

There are four general structures for writers' groups: 1) college style, 2) living room/café, 3) studio/writing center, and 4) online.

1.  **College-style groups** are modeled after graduate school writing classes. A leader sets meeting times and keeps the group on task. Copies of manuscripts are distributed to members to read and critique in advance of the meeting. This approach is especially helpful to novelists who would like to have longer segments of their work critiqued at one time. It works well if all of the members of the group do the prereads and written critiques, and if they attend all of the meetings. If members are less dedicated, it can be extremely frustrating.

2. **Living room or café groups** tend to be more casual. They meet in members' living rooms or coffee shops or free space at a bookstore or library. One person may lead the group or members may pass the baton. The level of task orientation varies from serious to social and often changes over time. Members may or may not bring copies of work they wish to have critiqued. Membership is generally free, but a personal invitation may be required.

3. **Studio groups** meet at writing centers that offer a variety of workshops. I admit to a bias in favor of these groups because they are generally led by experienced writers who also teach, and they tend to be task-oriented. Members bring copies of their manuscript pages to feedback sessions and read their work aloud. The smaller the group, the more pages you can bring. Connection with the center gives you the opportunity to develop your craft and start building a network of writing friends. A fee helps cover expenses.

4. **Online group**s are growing in popularity. They range from casual chats to highly structured university programs. Advantages include easy access, reasonable (if any) fees, and the ability to gather a group from a wide geographical area. The lack of face time is an advantage for some and a disadvantage for others.

## Is the Group Task Oriented or Primarily Social?

Both types have their place, but if you are looking for serious feedback, a task-oriented group is best. This is a group that's dedicated to helping members develop as writers. Rather than friendly chat about life and books, meetings revolve around manuscript reading and feedback. Guidelines ensure fairness and respect for individual members. The basic rule of a task-oriented group is to help each writer accomplish his or her goals.

## Does the Group Welcome Your Type of Writing?

Some groups welcome a variety of writers working on a variety of projects. Writers bring in everything from poetry to novels to articles to stage plays, and feedback reflects the varied experience of the members. If you have a strong leader who is also a generalist, you will learn a lot from him and the others in the group. Other groups are genre specific. Members write for particular markets such as children, young adults, literary or mainstream fiction, nonfiction, romance, horror, fantasy, poetry, or plays. Leaders of these groups are likely to know a fair amount about how to write for and get published in your chosen field. If you are passionate about a specific genre, a group like this might be right for you.

## Does the Group Serve the Members or the Organizer?

You'd think all writers' groups exist to serve the members. Most do, but now and then you come across one that exists primarily to serve the organizer, to give that person another feather in his hat. All you have to do to protect yourself from this is to be alert to the possibility. Look at the website and newsletters. Do you see news of members' successes or mostly news about the organizer and just a few of the members? The best groups are made up of good cheerleaders. They not only critique, they encourage fellow writers.

## Does the Group Have a Good Leader?

It's the leader's job to keep the group on task. She should see to it that everyone is treated fairly and reasonably encouraged. If a writer gets out of line (this happens, but rarely), it's the leader's job to deal with that person. This leaves everyone else in the group free to focus on the writing.

The ideal leader is passionate about writing and committed to helping you. Passion acts like a magnet. A person who has long loved writing will have learned a lot about it as s/he read, wrote, screwed it up, got it right, broke the pencil, and tried again. This person may or may not be extremely well published—it's the passion, the study, the urge to help people learn, that makes a good teacher.

The leader needs to be strong enough to keep the group on an even keel. She controls timing and moderates the feedback and the interaction among members so that you can be at ease. She also finds ways to challenge you (politely) when needed.

To see if a leader is committed to helping others, watch to see if she is truly delighted when a writer in the group makes a breakthrough—fixes a tough lead, brings a character to life, gets an agent for that first novel. If she is delighted, you are in the right place. On the other hand, if she deflects the conversation to her own successes or shows the teeniest bit of jealousy, even jokingly, bail out as soon as possible and find another group. You need a person who will help you, one you can trust to have your interests at heart.

## Do You Feel Welcome?

I recently led a writers' retreat at which most of the participants were returnees and knew one another. One of the few new people said, "I feel like there's a clique." Writer Barbara Malcolm looked at her and said, "There is, and you are part of it." That's how you should feel—as if there is a clique and you are part of it. This might take two or three visits, but it shouldn't take a year.

## Is Membership Limited So Everyone Gets Feedback?

I think the ideal number of members is six to twelve. Fewer than six and the energy drops off. More than twelve and it's hard to get enough time for critique. You can have more members if they tend to write shorter pieces or attend some meetings without bringing work.

## Are Writers in the Group Successful?

"Successful" means accomplishing what a writer wants to accomplish. Success may be writing for New York publishers or for grandchildren. The point is that successful writers actually work on their projects and complete them. If you happen upon a group of whiners, get out. The last thing you need when you are trying to make something of yourself is a cadre of people who say it can't be done.

## Is There Enough Expertise in the Group to Challenge You?

Being in a group that's just a half-step ahead of you is a good idea. You don't want to feel like a tag-along, nor do you want to be so far ahead of the others that they don't challenge you. I like the energy in mixed groups—with writers who are more experienced and just beginning, skilled in one area and not so skilled in others.

Some groups require that you submit a manuscript for approval before you are allowed to join. I've never seen that work well, because it's the nature of writers to write well one day and not the next. One manuscript tells you very little. College prerequisites are just about as iffy. Nothing annoys me more than the MFA grad who knows all there is to know about writing but very little about getting along with others. On the other hand, when writers in my roundtables noticed that members who took the Shut Up & Write! course not only improved quickly but were more fun to have around, they suggested making the course a prerequisite, even for very experienced writers. For us, that was a good plan because new members came into the groups speaking the same language and had a stronger understanding of the craft and the process. The level of competence in the roundtables—and the number of publications—increased almost instantly.

## Is the Critique Process Fair and Supportive?

The leader sets the tone and manages the conversation so members can stay focused on the craft. Time is balanced so that members receive fairly equal attention. Appropriate questions for the leader to ask other members include: Does the writing engage you? Did you get lost anywhere? What do you see that you absolutely love? Do you see any places where the writer has an opportunity to make this even better?

People in the fairest, most supportive groups occasionally make comments that sting. There's no way around an accident, but deliberate meanness is never warranted. Truthfully, I rarely see a writer get mean in my groups. And I never see them do it twice.

## Do You Feel Comfortable?

It might take a few meetings for you to decide whether or not you feel comfortable. You may always be nervous when presenting your work, but in a good group, people critique one another with respect, and that will eventually ease your mind. If, overall, you get useful feedback and feel at home, then you found the right place.

# How to Get and Give Useful Feedback

There are two sides of the coin in a writers' group: you get and you give. You get feedback when you share your work with the other members, and you give feedback when they share with you. Each side of the coin is rewarding. You learn as much about writing when you try to help others as you do when they are helping you. It's worth your while to attend meetings whether or not you have work to share.

## The "Get" Side of the Critique Coin

Feedback protocol varies from place to place. The procedures that I use in feedback sessions will serve as a good baseline for what you might expect (see Figure 25).

You may be asked to bring a copy of your manuscript for each member of the group. Follow the group's guidelines regarding the maximum number of pages. (For a manuscript format, see Appendix A.) If you do not have enough copies, the readers can share, but you will receive less written feedback.

When you arrive, put your name on the readers' list, and note the number of pages you wish to read. If you want to use your time to discuss a writing problem, write "talk" instead of a page count. When it's your turn, distribute copies of your manuscript and tell—in just a few words—the type of work. For instance:

- First chapter of a novel
- Short story
- Personal essay
- Article
- Poem for a collection
- Play
- Meditation/reflection

If you are midway in a book, you can attach or give a short synopsis—no more than a paragraph. Keep it brief so you don't use up your time explaining details.

Some teachers recommend telling the group what type of feedback you want, such as: "Do the characters seem real?" or "Is the story interesting?" I think directions like this often get in the way of good critique because readers will focus on the question, possibly missing another insight that would have been extremely helpful to you.

# Guidelines for Participating in Critique Sessions

## To Get Feedback on Your Writing

- When it's your turn, tell the type of work: first chapter of a novel, short story, personal essay, article, poem for a collection, play, or meditation/reflection.

- Don't explain. Don't apologize. Just start reading.

- When you're finished, take a deep breath while others make a few notes.

- Let the leader guide the feedback session. This is your time to sit back and listen.

- Wait until later to decide which suggestions you will use and which you will ignore.

## To Give Feedback to Other Writers

- When others read, notice what you think worked well.

- Also notice what you think might be better.

- Focus on the craft rather than the subject matter.

- Make as many notes for the writer as you can. Phrase comments in the first person, as "I think" or "I didn't understand" or as a question, rather than "You should. . . ."

- Join in the discussion when you want to. Say what you think, but don't insist. When there is disagreement about a certain point, the leader might ask for a show of hands so the writer can get the reaction of the whole group and can factor that into his decision.

- Remember that no one is expected to do as you say, only to consider your suggestions.

Figure 25.  Guidelines for Participating in Critique Sessions

In my groups, participants read their work aloud while the others follow along (and make notes) on their copies. Giving the readers two modes of input—auditory and visual—increases their level of attentiveness, which in turn increases the quality of feedback. You might find it uncomfortable to read your work aloud, but it does get easier with time and the benefits are well worth it.

Sometimes, just before they read, the most accomplished, competent writers get an urge to apologize for their work. With their permission, I posted a list of excuses on the Redbird website.

"This is the beginning of something longer."

"This is a possible first draft."

"This is just a continuation of something I started."

"I had to bring something 'cuz I wanted to come."

"This is the first draft of the possible start, or it could appear in the middle."

"I hope this measures up to my usual standard of mediocrity."

The last one, about the writer's "mediocrity," is from an award-winning novelist with four published books under his belt.

When publisher Philip Martin saw the list, he asked to include it in an anthology for writers. And thus, the Redbird list of snappy introductions became a chapter in *The New Writer's Handbook: A Practical Anthology of Best Advice for Your Craft and Career.*

The moral of the story: If you get the urge to apologize, don't. Pull out all of your teenage drama skills and fake it—pretend you are supremely confident. Sit up straight, speak clearly, and read as if everyone in the room is dying to hear what you wrote.

When you are finished reading, take a deep breath and wait for your heartbeat to slow down while the others make notes on your manuscript. After what seems like a century, the leader will open the conversation. Resist the urge to join the conversation, even if someone asks you a question. Every minute you speak is a minute during which you can't listen. It's a missed opportunity. You can hear what you have to say any time; you can't hear what these good readers have to say maybe ever again.

Some comments will please you; some will annoy. Some may make you want to start swinging. Be cool. You do not need to do anything right now, and you don't have to take any of the suggestions. You are the writer. You own the writing. You don't need to defend or argue. Take the manuscripts home with you, read the written suggestions, and think them over.

Often the suggestion that sounds brilliant at first sounds awful later, and the one that sounds awful turns out to be brilliant. Ask any accomplished writer and she will tell you a story of a time she wanted to choke a reviewer and had to admit, eventually, that the reviewer was right. My nemesis was a professor who said one of my stories was just like "the drivel written by every other divorcée in America." He deserved to die for the way he said it, but the truth is, he was right. It took me months to realize that. It would have taken me less time had I not wasted so much energy planning his demise. He eventually apologized and made up for it by coaching me through the writing of an award-winning article.

Whether you are a pro or a beginner, becoming a member of a critique group is likely to mark a turning point in your writing life. Carol S., a member of one of

Judy Bridges reviews comments made by members of her critique group.

my workshops, phrased it this way: "For years, I wrote in a safe and non-threatening room of my own, but with no outlet, I wasn't going anywhere. I took a chance on Redbird Studio. Although it was scary to 'get naked' in front of a room full of strangers, it was the best move I made. It's sheer luxury to have a coterie of able readers who show up regularly to give me feedback on my writing. Redbird has become a word synonymous with support and encouragement in my life. I feel very lucky to have discovered it."

## The "Give" Side of the Critique Coin

This is a case in which you'd think it would be easier to give than to get, but the truth is that writers often find it difficult to give feedback about another writer's work. When you critique a manuscript, you need to notice what you like and what you think might be improved, and you need to find a way to say so without making the writer want to deck you.

The good news is that the process is an immense learning opportunity for you as well as the person whose work you are critiquing.

As for how to say things, there is no substitute for an encouraging note written in the margin. "I love this" or "You really got me curious" can give a writer enough energy to make it through three more rewrites. When I'm short on time, I use my own shorthand to make notes on a manuscript. A single underline means "I like this." A double underline means "I love this." A scribbled, wavy underline means "I wonder about this."

Appropriate comments begin with "I." This signals that you are taking responsibility for your statement. Rather than saying, "Character is shallow," say, "I think this character needs more development." It takes but a second longer to add "I think" or "I wish," but that small touch makes the writer less defensive, more able to take in the meaning of your words.

The "sandwich" style critique is frequently recommended, but it can be a bit cumbersome. In the sandwich critique, each participant is expected to mention: something good, something that may need attention, and then another something good.

The trouble is, that's a lot of mentioning, especially if everyone in the group takes a turn. Most writers I know can handle, and indeed seek, deeper feedback than they can get with this method. I think the trick is to make sure that when you add up the comments made by all members of the group, the support is strong enough for this particular writer. Some people need more positive feedback; others want more critique. It doesn't take long for people to sense which way to go. The leader keeps her finger on the pulse and shifts the conversation if needed.

The worst thing is to write something snotty in the margin of a manuscript. It is not necessary, ever, to write "Duh" or "This sucks." Instead write "I wish I knew more about this" or "I wonder if a six-year-old would react this way" or "Did they have disposable diapers way back then?"

When you critique, it is essential that you focus on the craft rather than the philosophical content. In every group, there are people with varying political and religious opinions, and you are not going to agree with every one, all the time. It may not be easy to set your feelings aside, but you must. Some of my hardest days are when I help a person make a political point that annoys me. It's my job, so I do it. Later, when it's published, I wonder, did I really help with this?

In a critique situation, it is your job to consider whether or not the writing achieves the writer's goal and if it does not, what might help. If, on occasion, you cannot do that, if you find the content unbearable, your options are to remain quiet or to take a walk to the bathroom.

On the lighter side, few groups bother checking grammar, spelling, or punctuation at this stage of development. If an error jumps out at you, you might circle it, but line editing is not the point of critique. If you happen to be good at it, you can help the writer later, after she has all the words in order. See Figure 26 for a list of things to consider when you critique.

Overall, the critique you offer springs from everything you ever learned about writing—in your life and in previous chapters—and is tempered by your insights and simple caring for the others in your group.

If there was ever a good time to remember the Golden Rule, this is it.

# The Shut Up & Write! Critique List
## Things to Consider When You Critique

**Action.** Is there enough of it to keep you interested? Is it presented vividly? Does any of it feel as if it was inserted to meet a quota of chase or bedroom scenes?

**Author.** Are there places where you can "hear" the author's voice behind the words, explaining too much or promoting her agenda?

**Characters.** Can you identify the character's desire? Is the narrative drive—the combination of desire and difficulties—sufficient to hold your interest? Does the character speak and act in character? Can you see a little bit of yourself or someone you know in each character?

**Clarity.** Can you understand "who's on first" and what's going on? Is the language clear, or did you get lost some of the time?

**Clichés.** Do you hear phrases that are too familiar? To spot clichés, look for phrases that fall out of your mouth automatically. "Her mind was spinning." "His heart stopped." "At this point in time." "It goes without saying."

**Conflict.** Are there enough difficulties to challenge the characters and the reader?

**Dialogue.** Does the dialogue sound real? Does each phrase move the story, or are there filler phrases that really don't add anything, such as "Oh, really?" or "Is that right?"

**Ending.** Is the ending satisfactory? Does it make sense in light of the story?

**Facts.** Do the facts ring true? If fiction, is it believable? If nonfiction, are sources noted?

**Interest.** Does the piece hold your interest? Does it slow down anywhere, or move too quickly? Are the characters engaging? Is there enough tension? Mystery?

**Lead.** Is it effective? Does it set the scene and make you want to keep reading?

**Logic.** Does the action occur in a logical sequence? Are characters, settings, situations presented in an order the reader can follow: near to far, low to high, now to then?

**Market.** If the writer mentioned a target market, does the piece address that audience? Are the language, the story, and the tone appropriate?

**Pacing.** Does the story move at a pace that appeals to you? Did you feel rushed at times, or impatient?

**Passive versus Active Voice.** Is the active voice used most of the time? "The room was filled with fire" is passive. It "tells." "Flames licked the ceiling" is active. It "shows."

**Plot.** Does one thing lead logically to the next? Is there enough conflict to hold a reader's interest? Do things happen that seem too convenient, too improbable?

**Point of View.** Does the point of view stay steady, or does it wobble? If the point of view changes, does it do so at appropriate places? Is the reader alerted to the change? Does the narrator dip into the minds of too many characters, too quickly?

**Rhythm.** Does the language have a beat that flows with the story? Do the words, phrases, and paragraphs create a rhythm that suits the action?

**Scenes.** Do they feel real and vivid? Do you feel the tension, the heat, the cold, the characters, and the action?

**Sensory Detail.** Is there enough sensory detail to make the characters and settings come alive? Can you see, hear, feel, taste, and smell the people and places?

**Setting.** Is each setting vivid enough for you to see, hear, feel, taste, and smell? When the characters are in that space, do you feel as if you are there with them?

**Tell.** Does the author "tell" things you wish she would "show?"

**Title.** Is the title appealing? Does it make you want to read the story? Does it hold up once you have read it?

**Tone.** Does the choice of language complement the mood of the piece?

Figure 26. The Shut Up & Write! Critique List

# Chapter Ten

# A HATFUL OF RABBITS
## When the Going Gets Tough

I have forced myself to begin writing when I've been utterly exhausted, when I've felt my soul as thin as a playing card . . . and somehow the activity of writing changes everything.

—Joyce Carol Oates, novelist

You don't have to suffer to be a poet. Adolescence is enough suffering for anyone.

—John Ciardi, poet, essayist

I want to live other lives. I've never quite believed that one chance is all I get. Writing is my way of getting other chances.

—Anne Tyler, novelist

BEYOND THE NUTS AND BOLTS OF LEARNING HOW TO WRITE, there is life. Babies cry, spouses cheat, parents get sick, bosses get crabby. Day in and day out, after the novel is finished, before the next poem is begun, the morning you wake up with great ideas and the night you're sure it's all over—you have to keep at it. Visits from the Muse are not guaranteed.

Life happens to experienced writers as well as beginners, and sometimes even good news can cause a dry spell. I remember seeing Victoria Hinshaw in the café at one of the old Schwartz Bookshops, a tense look on her face, fingers poised over her laptop. I knew exactly what she was thinking: "What in heaven's name made me think I could do this?" She had a book contract for three romance novels— one written, two somewhere out there in the ozone, completely out of reach at the moment. She did finish them, of course, plus another five novels and three novellas. But that day in the bookstore, she was a deer in the headlights.

Writing rarely happens as easily as we'd like. A. Manette Ansay said that her novel *Good Things I Wish You* was ten years in the making. In his book *Other Colors*, Nobel prize-winning author Orhan Pamuk talked about his life as a writer:

> . . . the greatest source of happiness, is to write a good half page every day. For thirty years I've spent an average of ten hours a day alone in a room, sitting at my desk. If you count only the work that is good enough to be published, my daily average is a good deal less than half a page. Most of what I write does not meet my own standards of quality control.

And as if writers aren't hard enough on themselves, imagine working for the owner of a public relations firm who insisted that his writers keep churning it out, no matter what. If he walked past an office and didn't hear the keys clicking, he banged on the door and yelled, "Get busy!" I've written under that kind of stress. It ain't a whole lot of fun.

Among my most cherished belongings is a poster given to me by a colleague, Richard Fraser, who knew what it was like to write no matter what.

### The Most Terrifying Thing in the World

A blank piece of paper.

Everyone who communicates in print faces it almost every day of their lives. It frightens the good ones and terrifies the great ones. Only the mediocre take it in stride.

The mediocre have very little trouble filling the blank piece of paper . . . and they are always satisfied.

The good ones fill the blank piece of paper with sweat . . . and sometimes they are satisfied.

The great ones fill the blank piece of paper with blood and a few tears . . . and they are never satisfied.

If you are searching for meaning in the printed word . . . look for the writer who is terrified by a blank piece of paper.

—Anonymous

If the blank page scares you, take it as a sign that you are doing something that really matters to you. Even the most accomplished writers phase in and out of confidence, in and out of energy, in and out of determination and competence.

We all write more junk than we'd like to admit. Most of us spend less time writing than we'd like to admit, and we spend half of that time staring at the screen, wondering, "What in heaven's name made me think I could do this?"

To be a lifelong writer, you need to find ways to cope with the on/off, up/down business of putting your thoughts in readable form. You need to find what works to keep you going, and know that what works one time might not work the next.

Basically, you need a hatful of rabbits.

## Rabbit #1: Stake Your Claim

During my dark nights, I think of Mrs. Engelhardt, the English teacher who was the first to write "What lovely writing!" at the top of one of my stories. I found that story a while ago, and the writing wasn't all that lovely, but it wasn't bad, either, and her encouragement stuck in just the right corner of my brain. If you ask a roomful of writers whether or not they had a parent or teacher or aunt who praised them, nearly all say yes. If you were encouraged, you can bet that you had decent adults in your life, and what they said was true. If they thought you would be a better singer than a writer, they would have said so.

I do not agree with the statement "If you write, you are a writer." That's too easy. You are a writer because you are drawn to it, because you want to communicate and you work hard at it. Chances are you've been collecting pens, pencils, and notebooks since you were a kid. You remember stories you wrote in elementary school. You took more books out of the library than you could read, and to this day, you always have a stack of books or periodicals begging for your attention. When you read, you notice how words are used. You catch symbolism and nuance. You love the rhythm of beautiful language and the way a paragraph can turn your heart. When you write, you love the feel of paper, the sound of a pen on it, the soft click of a keyboard, the wild joy of finally, *finally*, getting it right. If these things are true of you, you are a writer.

Laurel Landis, a runner-up for *Rosebud* magazine's Mary Shelley Award, said, "The biggest thing I've done is to identify myself as a writer. It took me years to do that. Coming to Redbird was instrumental in realizing that I am as much a writer as I am all the other things in my life."

Laurel didn't casually claim she was a writer simply because she picked up a pen and scribbled a few paragraphs. She had been writing for years, studying the craft, attending workshops, and although she wasn't published at that point, she had finished several stories and was submitting her work. She really was a writer as much as she was "all the other things" in her life. Saying it out loud, laying claim to the identity, was a legitimate, logical step—one that affirmed her work and encouraged others to treat her like the writer she is.

When you wonder if you're for real, you project a lack of confidence that makes others wonder the same. You live in a vicious circle of "can't write/never will/ought to quit/give it up/nobody else thinks I'm any good either!"

When the going gets tough, do this: Stand up straight and say with conviction, "I am a writer. And even if I'm stuck at the moment, I will keep going and the words will come. I'll nail it. You can bet on it!"

## Rabbit #2: Surround Yourself with Support

Every writer needs a circle of support—the right combination of good will and good things to help get through the difficult days. You need to surround yourself with people who understand what you're going through, friends you can count on for advice or sympathy or a politely phrased kick in the butt. These are the friends you contact to:

- Meet at a coffee shop and write for an hour
- Plan an outing to a favorite bookstore
- Attend a reading by a newly published author
- Attend a writing conference
- Set dates on which you will exchange a certain number of pages
- Agree on a daily allowance of two minutes to whine
- Meet up at a hotel for a weekend of serious writing

Writers Sheila, Robert, Laurel, Carol, and Pam meet on Saturday mornings. One brings a prompt for a writing exercise. They write to the prompt and exchange enough encouragement to keep them focused on writing for another week.

Marjorie Pagel wrote this vignette to the prompt: use the word "cliché."

> She thought, my whole life has been a cliché. I'm just a cardboard cut-out of so many other Lisa Mullarkeys, though with different names, up here in front of an unruly, uncaring group of fourth graders, try-ing to teach them something that will benefit their lives.
>
> But then she intercepted those thoughts with some others, a kind of argument with herself: No, what I am really aspiring to is having one of these unpromising students emerge to be a cardboard cutout of me teaching other fourth grade students who will be cardboard cutouts. A cliché at the head of this class teaching a cliché and urging her charges to be clichés.
>
> From that moment on, Lisa Mullarkey determined that she would march to the beat of a different drummer and—*there!* she caught herself. *Another cliché.*
>
> —From "Lisa Mullarkey" by Marjorie Pagel

Email is a great way for writing friends to stay connected. Yes, we can waste time on it, but it's pure joy to send that quick email to friends saying, "I finished it!" and hear back, "Hooray for you! I knew you would." Roi Solberg is one of my writing friends. We live in different towns but are in touch daily to say, "How's the book coming?" "Did you finish that chapter?"

If you're very lucky, you have a dear writing buddy who's always there for you. Two of my friends met for years, to write and share their work. When one became seriously ill, the other showed up at her bedside with a notebook and pen and said, "Let's just write."

Last year Jean Scherwenka gave me three Clairefontaine notebooks as a birth-day gift. Only another writer would understand how precious that is.

## Rabbit #3: Ditch the Glommers

Writing, like every other field, has its share of people who will suck the life out of you if you let them. When the going gets tough, you have to get rid of these people.

- **Glommers** are like the girl you met in sixth grade, the one who glommed onto you the first day of school and never let go. She's in a writing workshop now, waiting to latch onto you and become your new best friend. She wants to attend every class with you, including the writers' retreat where she thinks the two of you should share a room.
  **Risk:** Suffocation. **Cure:** Just say no.

- **Bookies** buy all the books on the "For Writers" shelf and drag them around in huge, heavy tote bags. They don't write, they just rattle on about all the books they've read and look at you haughtily if you have not read the books they adore.
  **Risk:** Feeling insufficient. **Cure:** Roll your eyes.

- **Decorators** spend all of their time creating the perfect work space— brand new computer, tidy desktop, handle on the coffee cup in perfect alignment with the planet Jupiter. A little *feng shui* is fine, but honey, you do have to write.
  **Risk:** Distraction. **Cure:** Dress ugly.

- **Junkies** are addicted to classes. Show a junkie a brochure about a writing conference on the moon and they're gone. The next thing you hear from them will be the full report about who they met and how much they got out of it, which is always more than you got wherever you went.
  **Risk:** Boredom. **Cure:** Sigh deeply.

- **Exercisers** write hordes of writing exercises and journal entries they believe will add up to something, someday. They tell you about all the funny/sad/serious/interesting tidbits they have stored in plastic boxes that they'd love for you to read, but they won't attend a class or get down to business.
  **Risk:** Giving away your time. **Cure:** Tell them to Shut Up & Write!

- **High Rollers** are similar to exercisers. They have the most amazing things all worked out in their heads, bestsellers worth a fortune, but they aren't going to share them because someone might steal their ideas. Try telling them that you can't copyright an idea anyway, that they have to actually write it, and they will tell you that the writing can come later because, after all, that's the easy part.

**Risk:** Irritation.  **Cure:** Say your agent is calling.

- **Queens and Kings** simply must be a little above everyone else at all times. They are pleasant until someone else's star shines—until another writer gets especially good feedback or has a story accepted for publication—then they imply that the praise was mistaken or the publication insignificant, or say something cute, like "Couldn't you just kill her?" Beware. "Couldn't you just kill her?" is not a joke, it's a warning signal.

  **Risk:** Getting stabbed in the back.  **Cure:** Run. Now.

- **Know-It-Alls** populate every profession. They know the best way to do whatever you're doing and will drive you nuts with detailed instructions. The worst part is that they actually expect you to do what they say.

  **Risk:** Acrimony.  **Cure:** Tell 'em to stick it.

## Rabbit #4: Go through Your Orchid File

What, you aren't keeping an orchid file? Well, then, start one. Take a file folder, a box, or a huge trunk and put your orchids in it. Orchids are things that remind you how wonderful you are: congratulatory notes, awards, photos of the skit you wrote for the company party, a thank-you note from a friend, the newspaper clipping from the soccer tournament, your graduation tassel, keys for the red convertible you worked your butt off to buy. And every paragraph that was ever published, anywhere.

When you're gloomy, it's hard to remember you ever did anything good. That's when you haul out your file and go through your orchids. If you find an especially affirming news clipping or quotation, print (and maybe even decorate) it to hang on the wall near your computer. Or get a bulletin board and tack up some of your favorites. Call it your kudo-board. If you're going through a really bad phase, redo the kudo-board hourly.

The idea is to remind yourself of your beautiful moments. You can't count on others to do this for you—they may not even know you're gloomy.

## Rabbit #5: AC-cent-tchu-ate the Positive

Remember the song? "You've got to AC-cent-tchu-ate the positive, E-lim-in-ate the negative." Johnny Mercer wrote the lyrics in 1944, eight years before Norman Vincent Peale wrote *The Power of Positive Thinking*. It stands with others on the list of great tunes to listen to when you get the blues. On bad days, my mother would belt out "Everything's Coming Up Roses" right along with Ethel Merman. I swear, she could grit her teeth and sing "roses" at the same time.

Don't get me wrong, I'm all for screaming and crying when bad stuff happens. But soon enough I get tired of it and want to move on. Then it's time to AC-cent-tchu-ate the positive.

One way to do that is with affirmations. These are perfectly positive statements framing your world, your way. You can find a ton of them in books or online, or you can make up your own, or you can borrow one of these:

- I write quickly, easily, and well.

- I write interesting, exciting stories that hold a reader's attention.

- I see myself in a bookstore, signing copies of my new bestseller.

- I am free to write what I please, in a style that's all my own.

- I have more fresh ideas than I know what to do with.

- I thoroughly enjoy being a writer.

- Damn, I'm good!

## Rabbit #6: Hire a Dutch Uncle

A friend warns me that some people might take offense at this title. Apparently "Dutch Uncle" dates back to a time when the English and Dutch didn't like each other very much and the English used "Dutch" as a derogatory label. "Double Dutch" meant gibberish. "Dutch courage" was booze-induced bravery. A "Dutch wife" was a prostitute. "Dutch treat" is still used when you invite a person to dinner and expect them to pay for their own meal.

A "Dutch Uncle" is a practical, well-meaning, bossy guy who gives you grief when you need it. When it comes to writing, a Dutch Uncle is a man or woman you hire (or just ask) to give you grief if you don't do your work.

Tom Hanratty, for example, asked me to help him stay focused on a book he wanted to write. I said, "At the end of each month, you will give me a brown envelope with the pages you wrote that month. I will not read them, I just need to know you did the work." I promised that if he did not give me pages, I would say plenty about his irresponsible behavior.

I never got to say it. He turned in pages every month and eventually finished *The Art and Science of Tracking Man and Beast.*

I have a Dutch Uncle for this book, Susan Pittelman, who, after any period of silence, sends me an email that says, "Well?"

It works.

In another form of Dutch Uncle-ism, an unemployed playwright in one of my workshops whined and whined about how he couldn't get anything done. One night, while I was driving him home from a workshop, I asked if he had any money.

"Twenty bucks."

"Can I have it?"

"I guess, if you really need it."

He fished out the twenty and handed it to me, slowly. I stuck it in my pocket and said he could have it back when he wrote thirty pages.

In one week, he wrote thirty pages.

You can find a Dutch Uncle—any outspoken person whose opinion you respect. Work out an arrangement that keeps your feet to the fire.

## Rabbit #7: Do It Anyway

Like every writer, I'm certain I could write better, be more prolific, get more published, *if only* . . . If only I had more time, fewer interruptions, more encouragement, fewer worries, faster fingers, the perfect balance of inspiration, location, tools, and energy. Plus a personal assistant and a full-time massage therapist.

I can pile up excuses with the best of them, and I will argue long and hard for making a clear decision not to write during certain phases of life or the moon. With all that said, I know that if I really need to, I can do it anyway.

Anna Akhmatova, a Russian poet, lived through the Russian Revolution, the Nazi siege of Leningrad, and Stalin's terror. Her first husband was executed by firing squad, her third died in a prison camp. When her son was jailed, she stood with other mothers outside Leningrad's stone prison daily for seventeen months. Anna wrote a poem about it titled *Requiem* that became a popular epic. After that, she was expelled from the Union of Soviet Writers, her apartment was bugged, and the KGB kept watch on her friends and activities. Her work was banned. She wrote most of her poems while sitting on a window ledge. Her friends memorized them, and then she burned the poems in an ashtray.

I think about Anna when "I can't." And I reread an article that appeared in a January 1996 issue of the *Chicago Tribune* about a guy named Paul Adams.

> For eight hours every day, Paul Timothy Adams slumps in his wheel-chair before a computer screen at the Manor Care Nursing Home. A bright blue jawbreaker-sized ball rests under his lower lip, on his chin bone. The ball acts as Adams' mouse and connects to a handle, leading to a stand with a cable running to his laptop computer.

Adams was born with cerebral palsy. He was forty-three when the article was published. He had one book published, another under consideration, and another in the works.

Still want to complain because your computer crashed? Or because you're just too depressed to write?

My junior year in high school, Sister Mary Grace gave me a staff position on St. Clara Academy's award-winning journal, the *Sinsinawan*. Shortly after that, my little brother died from a congenital heart problem. I was devastated. When it was time to turn in my pages, all I had was a bunch of scrambled excuses—family problems, too much homework, I tried, but . . .

SMG stood staring down at me (she was at least a foot taller) and said that if I couldn't turn my work in on time, there was no point in having me on the staff.

I remember trying to glare at her hard enough to make her crumble.

Today I think the situation might be handled differently, that I might be given another chance. As it was, I learned a hard and lasting lesson: you do the job or you're out. I look at it as my Yoda moment. "Do or do not. There is no 'try.'"

When it comes to writing—as in so many other things—you either do it or you don't. The publisher can't print "trying." It doesn't matter whether your life is going right or wrong, whether you have the right kind of support or not. You own the pencil. You can choose to use it or not.

"Do or do not. There is no try."

## When You Put It All Together

Carol Wobig kept her mouth shut, first at home, where her sister did most of the talking, then in the convent, where silence wasn't mandatory although it was preferred, then in a pizza factory, where no one expected you to say much anyway. Throughout most of her adult years, Carol spread red sauce by day and wrote in her journal at night. The nearest she got to being rowdy was driving with two girlfriends to a new home in California.

Back in Wisconsin, in her fifties, she thought about her writing and decided it was time to take it seriously. She signed up for a writing workshop and was beset by the normal nervous worries: "What if they make me talk? What if I have to read my stuff?" They did, and she did, and nobody died. Thus began a whole new career for Carol.

You met her in earlier pages, when she fell down the stairs and her friends from the writing workshop were there to help her and to keep her going on the work she loved. One thing she missed, though, even after several of her stories were published, was her family's acknowledgment that what she was doing was pretty special. That changed when her workshop pals encouraged her to combine three monologues and submit them to a one-act play festival sponsored by

Village Playhouse of Wauwatosa, Wisconsin. When she won a place in the festival, her family came to see the production. She sat quietly, watching the stage. When the applause died down, her ninety-three-year-old dad turned to her and said, "I never knew you could do that."

Carol staked her claim, surrounded herself with support, focused on the positive, and "did it anyway."

CHAPTER ELEVEN

# SPIT-AND-POLISH

No passion in the world is equal to the passion to alter someone else's draft.

—H. G. Wells, novelist

Would you convey my compliments to the purist who reads your proofs and tell him or her that I write in a sort of broken down patois which is something like the way a Swiss waiter talks, and that when I split an infinitive, God dammit, I split it so it will stay split?

—Raymond Chandler, novelist

NOW THAT YOU'VE WRITTEN SOMETHING WONDERFUL and nursed it through critiques and a dozen rewrites, it's time to do the final edits. This is the spit-and-polish phase, when you go through the manuscript with the proverbial fine-toothed comb to make sure you have every *i* dotted and *t* crossed. Readers may forgive you for failing to describe the state of Connecticut, but they will not forgive you for spelling it wrong.

"What?" you say. "I wrote it. I did all the hard work. Now you want me to do the editing, too?"

Yes. That's exactly what I want you to do, and that's exactly what every agent, publisher, and contest judge wants as well. In an ideal world, you would send your "almost clean" novel to an agent, who would present it to a publisher, who would make you an offer you couldn't refuse and, after the deal was sealed, assign an editor who would fix it so no errors saw the light of day. In the real world, it's your job to see that the editing is done, and done well, before you send any type of manuscript anywhere.

I learned the importance of careful editing when an agent taught a workshop at my studio. He demonstrated the way he sorts through hard copy submissions.

In Pass One, he slits the envelope, draws the query or proposal pages halfway out and scans what is written on that first half page. If he sees typos or spelling or grammatical errors, regardless of the caliber of the writing, he slides the pages back into the envelope and drops it on the reject pile. Later an assistant will return the proposal to the writer, along with a nicely worded rejection. When the writers in our workshop gasped, the agent explained that he sees mistakes as a signal that "this writer doesn't care enough." To him, errors mean the writer might also be careless with facts or rewrites or critical deadlines. The agent has X amount of hours in the day to do his job, and he's not going to waste them on a writer who doesn't care enough to get it right.

Tough, huh? But true in almost all fields of writing. The editor of the online journal doesn't have much time, either. And no one likes using his precious minutes to fix another's mistakes.

## Should You Do the Editing or Get Help?

The answer to this is fairly simple. If you are weak in any area of the editing process, get help. If you are very good at it, you can do almost all of it yourself, but I'd still have another excellent editor make the last pass.

I am not a great editor. I can spot the developmental issues—the relationship that needs depth or the point of view that's dancing—but rules about commas and split infinitives elude me. I need help.

My first line of defense is my husband. He's one of the few people I know who can actually diagram a sentence. It's also an advantage that I know him well enough to know when his heart is not in the job. At those times, I beg friends for help. Sometimes payment is required, perhaps lunch or help with their writing project, or even cold hard cash. Whatever, it's worth it.

The next step is to hire professional help. Professional editors work at several levels, from the early stages when you need help thinking through the concept, through development of the text, and on to the final line edits. Chris Roerden, an independent editor and the author of *Don't Murder Your Mystery* and *Don't*

*Sabotage Your Submission*, says, "Everyone, even the professional editor, turns out clearer, more effective writing if someone else test-drives the draft, that is, if others review it before it is printed, posted on a blog, or otherwise submitted for publication."

# The Part You Do Yourself

Whether you are editing a letter to the editor or your *magnum opus*, there are logical steps in the process. I recommend that you go through the manuscript five times, each time focusing on a specific area. It's best to complete each step, following it all the way through the manuscript, before you go on to the next. This is like re-keying rather than a cut-and-paste revision—it sounds like it will take longer, but it actually takes less time because you do a better job of it.

Before you begin, let the manuscript rest for a while—a few days or weeks or longer—so you can look at it with fresh eyes.

### Pass One: Read Through

Pretend you are a stranger reading the manuscript for the first time. Are the names and places consistent? Are the scenes and events in the right order? Does everything make sense?

Make notes in the margins near sections you think need help. Don't stop to fix them now. Read it all the way through and then go back to do the fixing. You may have to let the manuscript rest and retrace this step a few times so you know you have the words in the right order before you go on.

### Pass Two: Grammar

This time, ignore everything else and just pay attention to the grammar. If something troubles you, make a mark in the margin and keep going. When you finish reading, go back and make the corrections.

### Pass Three: Spelling

Follow the same procedure with spelling. Read, circle questionable words, go back later to check and correct the spelling. One hazard with spelling is that we often believe the wrong word is the right word (affect and effect) so we don't see our mistakes. Watch for tricky items, such as using "compliment" when it should be "complement." If you question the usage, you can look it up in a style guide. For this purpose, I use the *Associated Press Stylebook* because it is easy to use and light enough to carry around. You can also use other style guides, or go online, or seek help from the friend who won the all-city spelling bee. (In a few paragraphs I'll talk about other style guides you might use.)

For prefixes and suffixes, I find a word book, the kind with thousands of spellings, to be more helpful than a dictionary.

And sometimes I do an online search, typing in the wrong spelling to see what comes back with the question: "Did you mean . . . ?" Yes, that's what I meant!

## Pass Four: Punctuation

Definitely use a style guide for punctuation. Different guides have different rules. Use the one that's appropriate for your publisher. There is a list at the end of this chapter.

## Pass Five: Outside Reader

Ask someone who has never seen the manuscript—one who does not know your message/theme/agenda—to read it through. See if this someone understands what you have written or catches any errors you missed. Many errors slip in at the last minute, when you make a correction that changes something else . . . and that something else is now so embarrassing you could die.

When fax machines were still popular, I prepped a flyer about a business writing class I was teaching. I put a fake sticky note on the front that said, "Do you know anyone who can use this?" A friend volunteered to design it on his computer and send it out overnight. When I walked into my office the next morning, there were several faxes in my machine. The top one was a copy of my flyer. The fake sticky note showed clearly, but instead of saying, "Do you know anyone who can *use* this?" it said, "Do you know anyone who can *us* this?" "Us" was circled, and alongside of it, there was the answer, printed in large black letters: "Yes. You!"

The fax had gone out to six hundred human resource directors.

Even if I had seen the flyer when it was ready to go, I might have missed the error. Obviously my friend missed it. A stranger, anyone who was unfamiliar with our project, would have caught it in an instant. And, oh, how I wished someone had.

## Style Guides

My list of "books you must have" is short. If you are like most writers, you already have a houseful. But if you don't have a style guide, get one. You can supplement and update information by looking online, but there's nothing quite like turning the pages of a style guide to remind you that you still have a lot to learn.

When it comes to grammar and spelling and punctuation, hardly anyone knows it all. Lay/Lie? Who/Whom? Does the comma go inside or outside of the quotation mark? When is a person's title capped? Is a book title still underlined? Are the rules the same in print as online? If you do not know the answers to all of these questions, forgive yourself—I know only three people in the universe who do and they are professional editors. For the rest of us, it is far better to own, and use, a style guide.

There are differences among the styles, including protocol for citation, so it is important to pick the guide that's appropriate for your field.

*The Associated Press Stylebook and Briefing on Media Law* (AP) is standard in the newspaper and magazine industries, and often used in advertising, marketing, and public relations. It is updated frequently and favored by many who attended journalism school because of the easy A-Z format and small size—this one fits in your backpack. It's perfect company at the bus stop, where you can flip through pages and answer questions you didn't know you had, such as whether or not you can abbreviate Governor, as in Gov. (Yes, with a capital G, if you use it before the name. No, if you use it after the name.)

One hazard with using *AP* style is that some rules differ from those in guides used for other publishing venues. For instance, the *AP* recommendation on commas is to use them to separate items but not before a conjunction, as in

"We came, we saw and we conquered." In contrast, *The Chicago Manual of Style* strongly recommends placing a comma before a conjunction, as in "We came, we saw, and we conquered."

*The Chicago Manual of Style* is the gold standard for most non-journalistic writing. Published in hard cover by University of Chicago Press, *Chicago* is the fat, heavy, comprehensive bible used by nearly all book publishers and some public relations and business communicators. It is updated less often than *AP*—approximately every ten years—but that lack is more than made up for by an excellent website. *Chicago* also emails periodic Q&A updates you can use to sharpen your editing skills. I get lost in this guide and hate carrying it around, but I have to admit it's the one I really should be using almost all of the time.

The *Publication Manual of the American Psychological Association* (APA) is commonly used for social sciences and other academic publications; however, many universities and academic organizations have other preferences or print their own guides.

In the *MLA Style Manual*, MLA stands for Modern Language Association. It is used by scholars, professors, graduate students, and other writers of scholarly books and articles, especially in the humanities such as English and other modern languages and literatures. It is also referred to as the *MLA Handbook* and the *MLA Style Manual and Guide to Scholarly Publishing*.

The *American Medical Association Manual of Style* (AMA) is a guide for medical publications. Oxford University Press and *JAMA* Archives (Journal of the American Medical Association) sponsor an online version of the manual.

*The Elements of Style* simply must be mentioned, although it is not as comprehensive as the other guides. This is the tiny book you met in school and possibly still love and carry around with you. Otherwise known as "Strunk & White," for its authors William Strunk Jr. and E.B. White, it was first published in 1918; revised editions have been released several times since then. My favorite version, *The Elements of Style Illustrated*, was designed and illustrated by Maira Kalman and published in 2005. Imagine, a grammar book with pictures. You gotta love it.

*Wired Style: Principles of English Usage in the Digital Age* is a guide to online usage. This pocket-sized manual deals with how you talk about cyberspace: is it E-mail or email, Internet or internet?

*The Yahoo! Style Guide: The Ultimate Sourcebook for Writing, Editing, and Creating Content for the Digital World* covers the basics of grammar and punctuation as well as topics with a web-specific focus. It includes word lists (and the suggestion that you make up a word list of your own) plus information about search engine optimization, user interface text, and eye tracking so you can shape your text for the web. *The Yahoo! Style Guide* is available in print and online.

## For Your Reading Pleasure

A full citation for each of these style guides is included in the References (see page 163).

# Chapter Twelve

# GETTING PUBLISHED
## It's a New Day

After many seasons of study and contemplation (sitting lotus on my mountain of rejection slips), after years of talking to and dealing with scores of editors (and being an editor myself) I have discovered something momentous—nothing less, ladies and gentlemen, than the secret to getting published.

Are you ready?

Here it is: write something good.

That's it. Simple as that. Good writing. That's all an editor wants. And the fact that every editor is going to define the simple phrase in a different way is not a problem, not really. If you're making good writing—fresh, important, well-made, compelling, top-of-the-line stuff—someone out there is going to want to publish it.

—Bill Roorbach, from *Writing Life Stories*

EVERYWHERE YOU TURN, YOU HEAR BAD NEWS about the publishing business. You hear how the grand old publishing houses are closing their doors or consolidating; periodicals are going out of print; newspapers are folding; the only authors getting published are the top few, sure-fire money-makers; it's all about who you know, and the little guy, the new author, doesn't stand a chance.

Before you let the bad news get to you, take a walk in a bookstore. Look at the endless rows of books and periodicals filled with page after page of words. Writers filled those pages—men and women who bent over their keyboards, wrote, deleted, groaned, grinned, and bonked themselves on the head just the way you do. They worked hard at writing and at getting their work published. And there it is, in row after row. . . .

If you want to get your work published, you have to:

1. Write well

2. Study the markets

3. Understand the process

4. Be creative

# 1. Write Well

Non-writers often underestimate what it takes to become an author. I get calls from people asking me to put them in touch with an agent. Nine times out of ten these people haven't written a thing, they just have an idea for a bestseller they think is going to earn them a million. When I ask about the writing, they say, "How hard can it be?"

These are not my favorite conversations.

People who take writing seriously know that it takes years of practice to learn how to write well, and another two to five years to author a book that's worth the trouble of publishing. True, there are a few lucky stiffs who blurt out a winner and make it all look easy, but the rest of us mere mortals have to pay our dues. We study books like this one, practice, practice, practice, and finally figure out how to "write something good."

Every agent/editor/publisher who has a space wants to fill it with something good. When you pay your dues, when your work is truly good, it stands out above the rest. You will be the tall guy in the line of basketball picks.

# 2. Study the Markets

The first place to look for markets is your own bookshelf. Look at the things you like to read. You know much more about those things than you think— length, tone, style. You almost naturally write in a manner that's appealing to those markets. You know what people are looking for because that's what you read.

Market guides such as the *Writer's Market* series are also good starting points. The printed guides offer you the luxury of paging through well-organized listings in various categories. Make sure you do two things with the printed market guides:

1.  Read the first chapters. You will find them filled with some of the best, most current information about the industry, as well as tips on such things as query preparation and rates to charge for various writing jobs.
2.  Always double-check the details. When you find an attractive listing, go to that publication's website to read current writer guidelines and check editors' names and addresses.

Online market guides offer the advantage of targeted searches and more up-to-date information. Again, double-check what you learn by searching publisher websites. Take notes and set up a system to keep track of possibilities.

## Markets for Shorter Work

General and targeted periodicals

Newspapers

Newsletters

Literary magazines

Anthologies

Contests

Internet publications

To focus your market search on possibilities for shorter works, reach beyond the guidebooks and your bookshelf. Search the Internet. Look around town, especially at whatever venue is the best source for periodicals. This might be a bookstore, but may also be a corner newsstand. In my area, it's a hobby shop that carries more magazines than any place else in the city. On one visit, I counted 22 literary and 132 computer magazines. On another, I tested the topic "Victorian" and found six magazines I could look through to determine whether or not a piece I wanted to write was appropriate.

When you find publications that look like possibilities, study the cover copy and the ads—are they targeted to a particular age or education or interest group? Read the editor's notes and letters to the editor. Look at sections to see if one might be more accessible than others. Editors often welcome new writers in smaller sections like "city lites" so they can get to know them before assigning full-length features. Read first and last lines of articles and stories. Check length, tone, style. Take notes.

Your writing group is a good resource for information about literary and academic publications. Almost every literary magazine today has an online presence. Also look in libraries and campus book stores. Be alert to submission schedules because many have long lead times. Pay may be skimpy, but what you lose in bucks you earn in cachet.

For newspapers, to the top dailies in town, add the smaller weeklies and special-interest publications. More than one good writer earned her stripes—and clips and discipline—writing for the weekly shopper.

Newsletters and in-house magazines designed for business and nonprofit organizations offer interesting, although less visible, opportunities. Business groups generally pay. They are easier to reach if you have a business background. For nonprofits, you may wish to start your market search by thinking of your interests and backtracking to groups related to those subjects. Do you belong to any special interest groups? Do they have small magazines or newsletters? Could they use a one-time story or article, or maybe a column? One of the first pieces I had published was a Mother's Day story that found a home in a small association magazine called *Health and Wealth*. Pay: Twenty bucks, plus all the encouragement I needed to keep going.

Anthologies are perfect showcases for shorter works, especially short stories, creative nonfiction, personal essays, and inspirational writings. Look for anthologies in libraries and book stores. Calls for submission are listed online, in market guides, and in the writer magazines. Read guidelines carefully for the publication's specific focus and requirements. Some showcase contest winners, or a selected "best of," and are not open to general submissions. Others take nearly everything they get their hands on. Read the anthology. See if you will be proud of the company you're keeping. Do not, however, pay to have your work included. You can check out publications online at sites dedicated to identifying predators, or do an online search for "[name] complaints" to protect yourself.

Internet publications of all genres welcome submissions. Most do not pay, but more and more are becoming highly respected. This can be a little tricky since the 'net is also full of poorly edited, poorly written pretenders and scam artists. The best guide is your own reading eye. Don't believe what they say about themselves—take the time to read material on the site. If it's up to your standard, it's where you want to be.

Keep watch for fresh opportunities on the web and elsewhere. New things are happening all the time, and if you're on top of it, you'll be first in line.

## Markets for Book-length Work

Agencies

Big houses/divisions

Mid-sized and small presses

Self-publishing, including Print on Demand (POD)

The first stop for most book writers is to look for agency representation. The agent represents the author to publishers, so the one you want—if you can get 'em—is the one who has had success with writers in your field, who knows key publishers well enough to contact them and get attention for your book. Your perfect agent will be excited about working with you, also smart and savvy enough to make good deals with the publishers.

You pay the agent out of royalties, which means she is not going to get rich until you do, which means she is very selective about which writers she takes on, which means that getting an agent isn't easy. Some people have luck with the guide books. Others meet through friends, or at conferences, or through web searches. Wherever you get the names, research carefully to find names of writers they have represented (you want to know if you fall in that line or not) and whether or not they are welcoming new clients. Avoid agents who charge for reading your work or who try to sell you on buying editing services from them.

Few of the big name publishers are willing to accept un-agented submissions. You need to know about the companies and their divisions, and know who publishes books of your type, but direct contact will be limited until after an agent has kindled the fires.

Mid-size and small presses tend to be more accessible. Writers often enjoy working with them because the contact is more personal and the writers have more say in the publishing process. The trade-off is that there is less status associated with a smaller press. Also, marketing budgets are generally limited. If you are comfortable with the fact that marketing budgets are limited for all but (and maybe including) big-name authors, this will seem less of a loss to you. Few publishers of any size are paying for fancy ad campaigns and book tours these days. The bulk of the marketing falls on the author, at the author's expense.

Self-publishing used to be considered the last resort of authors who could not get their books published elsewhere. Today self-published books vary from dreadful to extremely well-written and respected. You can track the history of attitudes toward self-publishing by looking at the Council for Wisconsin Writers annual contest rules. For years, self-published books were not accepted in the competition. Then, in 2006, Paul Salsini submitted his World War II novel *Cielo,* and against stiff competition, won the Anne Powers Fiction Book Award. Clearly, whatever people thought about self-publishing in the old days, it's a whole new ball game.

There are great reasons to self-publish. You can control the presentation of your book, collect a larger percentage of each sale, and have the book you want even if the market for it is quite small. Sales are up to you, so don't do it unless you either can sell the book, or don't care whether or not it sells.

Methods vary from having your book coil bound at the local copy center to having small or large runs produced by an online Print-on-Demand (POD) service, to publishing an e-book for distribution on the web or an e-reader, to having it professionally designed and printed in hard cover. The industry is changing every twenty minutes as new services come on the scene. The process can be fun and exciting and profitable, but before you invest in anything you are not

100 percent sure of, study guidebooks such as Dan Poynter's *The Self-Publishing Manual,* and talk to authors who have self-published successfully.

## 3. Understand the Process

You need to learn about the business of publishing. Bah, you say. I'm a writer, not a business person. Well, sadly, no agent or publisher is going to creep into your studio at night and pull your perfect manuscript out of the file. You are going to have to figure out how to get it in front of the people who can do you some good. They might or might not buy it, but if you sit there with your feet up, waiting for someone else to do it for you, it is absolutely not going to happen.

Make it a habit to look at the world from the other side of the desk, from the point of view of the people you want in your corner. If you were the editor of a periodical, how would you respond to a writer who sends a full manuscript when you've asked for queries, who can't seem to spell or punctuate, or who suggests stories that don't belong in your publication? Are you going to assign another story to a writer who was late last time, or who called three times to complain about a paragraph you left out of his last too-long story?

In writers' guidelines and market listings, gatekeepers tell us what they want to see. "Query only," "First ten pages," "No personal essays." The best way to annoy the people you want on your side is to ignore their requests. Editors repeat, time after time, "Read the publication before you submit," and yet they receive untold numbers of submissions that just don't fit—sometimes from the same writers. One writer repeatedly sent erotic stories to a Christian literary magazine. After several form rejections, "Not for us" and a polite "Please. We are a Christian publisher," the editor finally sent a boldly printed note: "Don't you dare send any more of your stories!"

Mistakes happen to the best, most conscientious writers, but they make as few errors as possible for their sakes and the sake of fellow writers. Those who screw up ruin it for others. How long, for instance, do you think it will be before the editor of the aforementioned Christian publication says to the market guides, "Take me off your list! You wouldn't believe the things they send me!"

Publishing is a complicated business, demanding on the people who are in it and those who are trying to get in. Agents, editors, and publishers all work hard, and they expect writers to work hard, too. They want to have something good to show for their hours of hard work, and regardless of the jokes, tormenting writers is not enough. You can complain all you want in private—that's part of the game—but at the end of the day, you will have a better chance of getting published if you can see the business from their side of the desk.

## The Two Paths to Publication

The marketing process gets confused in workshops when facilitators give instructions based on their own writing backgrounds. The person who writes fiction says to write the story first and then submit it; the person who writes nonfiction says you should always have a contract before you begin writing. The truth is, there are two different paths to publication, one for things you need to write first, and one for the things you can sell first. There is a summary of the two paths in Figure 27 (page 152).

| **Things You (Generally) Write First** | **Things You (Generally) Sell First** |
|---|---|
| All stories, fiction and nonfiction | Articles |
| Creative nonfiction | Profiles |
| Historical fiction | Biographies |
| Reminiscence | Business |
| Memoirs | Marketing |
| Personal essays | Self-help |
| Humor | How-to |
| Inspirational | Histories |
| Poetry | |
| Opinion | |

## The Write-First Path to Publication

The "write-first" path to publication includes all of the stories you write—short and book length—whether they are fiction or nonfiction. In earlier chapters, we talked about how a story is a story is a story whether it's fiction or fact. You use the same techniques to write your glorious novel as you do to write the saga of your grandmother's march across the tundra. In both cases the agent, editor, publisher, or contest judge needs to see the actual writing in order to make a decision.

The write-first path is appropriate for all types of writing in which the phrasing matters most. You can say a piece is humorous, but an editor can't tell whether it's really funny without reading it. You need to actually read a personal essay, creative nonfiction, historical fiction, reminiscence, memoir, opinion, inspirational, or poem in order to appreciate it.

If you are as well known as, say, Stephen King, you can tip a glass with your publisher and say, "I'll write a comedy," and even if you've never written anything like it in your life, get the go-ahead. The rest of us have to write the funny stuff before it gets accepted.

### *The Write-First Path for Shorter Works*

**Finish writing the entire piece**

**Edit carefully**

**Check publication guidelines**

Read publication guidelines on the publisher's or agent's website and follow them to the *t*. They rule.

**Prepare a cover letter** (for a sample format, see Appendix B)

Some people think a cover letter is necessary; I think it's optional. You certainly can't hurt yourself by sending one. On the other hand, I think it looks a little silly if all it says is "Here is my manuscript." I would send one if I wanted to remind the editor of a prior contact or mention that my work has appeared in other publications.

### Prepare the manuscript

Follow publisher guidelines. For a standard manuscript format see Appendix A. Also check the latest edition of the Writer's Digest book, *Formatting & Submitting Your Manuscript.*

### Submit the full manuscript

Submit the full manuscript unless the publisher's guidelines say to do it another way. Follow directions for submitting online or by mail. Once upon a time, the rule was to never, ever submit a story to more than one place at a time. You sent the manuscript, waited for a response, then sent it to others one at a time. That wasn't too bad when editors had time to turn things around quickly (even though it still seemed like forever). Now it really is forever and waiting several months for one-at-a-time turnarounds is ridiculous. I can't imagine shopping for a car and having the sales rep say, "I'll hold it 'til next year while you decide," so why should a writer wait? Fortunately, more and more editors are accepting simultaneous submissions. Check the guidelines. If they say they want to know if this is a simultaneous submission, don't play games—tell them.

### Keep track of submissions

Online trackers are handy, but any system will do, even a paper clip on the top of a file folder. Just keep track of what you sent, where. If you can get a clue from the guidelines, note when you might expect a response.

### Follow-up

It's tough to figure out when to follow up and when to leave it alone. You can safely send an email a few weeks after the stated reading time. Ask if your submission arrived, if they've had a chance to look at it, and when a decision will be made. Most editors are gracious about responding—just remember that they are crazy busy and don't have time to respond to a dozen questions.

If you don't get a response as promised, follow up again in a few weeks.

**When you get a contract for print publication**

If you get a contract that says, "all rights" or "pays on publication," you have a decision to make. A popular anthology's contract agrees to pay on publication, but adds that publication may take up to two years, is not guaranteed, and the writer may not submit the work elsewhere during that time. I don't think I'd sign that one, but other writers do and have been very proud of publication when it happens.

The ideal is "one-time" rights (the right to use it, once) and "pays on acceptance," which is when they take it rather than when it's published. The truth is, we often compromise, especially if it's a nice publication. When the assistant editor of a news magazine called me to accept an essay I'd submitted, she asked, "Would $250 be all right?" I had to keep myself from saying, "I think I can afford that," as if I was going to pay her. I probably would have.

### *The Write-First Path for Book-length Works*

**Finish the book**

Unless you have a relationship with the agent or publisher, do not approach either before you have finished the book.

**Write your query letter**

The query is based on the finished manuscript—you are asking the agents/publishers/editors if they would be willing to look at the book you have already written. (See Appendix B for a sample format for your letter.)

The query letter is probably the most difficult writing you'll ever do in your life. Read every "how to" article and sample you can find, and plan on a few months of writing and rewriting to get your query right. You are rarely allowed more than one page in which to sell your concept, your writing, the book's marketability, and your ability to help sell it. Do not waste your breath saying this is the one book you just had to write. First efforts rarely make it big, so they'll want to know that you have plans for more.

If you know anyone who has had success writing queries for similar works, beg/pay them to help you, but never leave it all up to them. You need to do your own studying and follow your own star.

One bit of good news is that you can send several queries at a time. Make a list of potential agents and publishers, those who handle books similar to yours. Tailor each query, mentioning specific titles they handled and how your book fits into their market. At this point, you are asking them to take a look at your work. You can ask as many as you like at one time—five to ten is reasonable.

If you get a rejection, have a fit, throw a few things at the wall, then sit down and query the next prospect on your list.

**Have your full proposal ready to send**

Good news. The agent sees good things in your query. She might ask for fifty pages or three chapters or a full proposal. You will send what she asks for, of course. If it is for the full proposal, she will want all or parts of the following:

- **Cover letter:** A businesslike response to the agent's letter with a list of what you are including in the proposal package.

- **Title page:** A practically blank page with book title and author's name. Send if requested. Follow standard format.

- **Contents page:** Usually not sent with novels. But do include a contents page for a collection of any type.

- **Synopsis:** A very short (1-2 page) showcase of the book and your writing. Do your best to engage the reader in characters and plot, perhaps by leading with an excerpt from a vivid scene. Not a summary or "in this chapter" description of the book.

Tips: Write in present tense, regardless of the tense used in your manuscript. Start with a scene or statement of the tensions rather than telling the reader what you think they need to know about the background and characters. Keep it short.

- **Chapter outline:** Often a synopsis or a chapter outline is requested, sometimes both. If it's a chapter outline, show off your writing. Engage rather than describe.

- **Author biography:** The agent doesn't care where you were born. She wants to know what makes you the best person to have written this book. She also wants to know you can help sell it. Although this is not a marketing statement, if you can gracefully refer to elements of your platform—your social network, web presence, speaking experience, or marketing savvy—all the better.

- **First three chapters or first fifty pages:** Send what they ask for, no more, no less.

- **Endorsements (also known as "blurbs"):** These are testimonials that might appear on the back cover of the book when it is published. They are best when written by people who actually read the manuscript.

## The Sell-First Path to Publication

This path to publication covers things you usually think of as nonfiction or informational. With these works, the agent/editor/publisher bases her decision on your idea plus your proven or assumed skill as a writer. If you are a first-time writer, you may have to complete the writing so she can be sure you are capable. If you are an experienced writer, she'll look at your query or proposal, your track record, and her own needs for the agency or publication. She doesn't expect the writing to be finished at the time you propose your idea. She does expect you to have an excellent plan and a comprehensive list of marketing possibilities, especially for book-length works.

### The Sell-First Path for Shorter Works

#### Query

The query is basically a sales letter written to the publisher's gate-keeper, usually the editor of a magazine (online or print) or an editorial assistant. Your challenge is to keep it to one page that includes your concept, research, credentials, and a mini-writing sample.

See the latest edition of *Writer's Market* for up-to-date tips on writing query letters. (See Appendix B for a sample format.) The overall approach includes:

- An engaging lead, possibly the first few lines of the written piece

- Details fleshing out the lead

- Your credentials (what makes you the one to be writing this)

- Contact information

It is okay to submit queries simultaneously to non-competing markets, i.e., publications that are not distributed to the same readership. If you are sending the query via snail mail, be sure to include a self-addressed, stamped envelope (SASE).

#### Agreements

When an interested editor contacts you about your idea, you will discuss any specific requirements she may have concerning slant, length, resources, etc. Then you agree on a fee (again, see market guides for the latest averages and adjust to your region) and whether you will be working "on spec" or "on assignment."

- "On spec" means "on speculation." The term means that you write the article, submit it, and then the editor decides whether she will use it. In other words, "on spec" means "write it, we'll look at it." There is no promise to pay you for your work.

- "On assignment" means that you are writing with a firm assignment. Sources often ask if you are writing on assignment, especially if they are interviewed frequently and hesitate to spend time with a writer who is writing on spec, because there is no guarantee that the article will be published. If the editor kills an article you wrote on assignment, she may pay a "kill fee," a small fee to acknowledge your labor.

### Best Terms

Pays on acceptance rather than on publication. Pays a rate that seems fair for your region.

### Rights

The issue of rights is enough to drive a person crazy. In an ideal world, from the writer's point of view, the publication would agree to purchasing "one time" rights—the right to print your work one time and one time only. The "one time" might be the first time it's published (first rights) or the first time it's published in North America (first North American rights). Now that all or parts of a publication may be online, publishers frequently want "world rights." The argument bounces back and forth between the publisher saying, "I need world rights because we need to put everything online," and the writer saying, "If you need world rights, then pay me for them."

You can negotiate, but to do so you need to know what's legal and what's customary in your region, this week. This is another good reason to belong to a writer's group, in this case a group of savvy freelance writers. Do not depend on yesterday's information. Use your research skills to find out what's happening.

### *The Sell-First Path for Book-length Works*

### Query

As with shorter works, it is okay to send queries simultaneously to several agents or publishers. Make sure they are tailored to the specific agency. (More information on queries is on page 148.)

**Proposal**

Have your proposal ready to send when you receive a request, but check the agent's guidelines for specific requirements. A full proposal can include:

- Cover letter

- Title page

- Table of Contents

- Overview of book (short) or chapter outline

- Marketing information—a competitive analysis and ideas for promotion

- Author biography—your credentials

- Sample chapters or first fifty pages

- Endorsements—testimonials that would be appropriate on the back cover

**Contract**

Negotiate the contract with the help of your agent or attorney.

**Write the book**

## Oh, No. Not a Rejection!

One of the first real writers I met worked at her home on Chesapeake Bay. I spent a lovely afternoon there, sitting at a craggy picnic table, eating bouillabaisse cooked in a big black pot on an old, wood stove. After lunch, we took a walk around the little town, and as we passed the post office, the writer looked wanly at a trash can. "I threw a good manuscript in there," she said.

The manuscript was one of her first short stories. She had submitted it to *Reader's Digest*, which was publishing only reprints at the time. The day she opened her post office box and found her self-addressed, stamped envelope with a form rejection inside, she threw the envelope—story and all—into the trash. It was her only copy.

Years and many publications later, she still thinks about that story.

You do not submit your only copy of a story, ever. But if (when) you get a rejection, you might, as she did, feel the urge to yell, "Screw it!" and walk away from the whole business of writing.

Fine. Do that for a while. Go to bed and whimper for a week. You don't have to get over it immediately—we are, after all, human beings, and if we liked rejection all that much, we'd ask more gorgeous people for dates. Few among us can toss a rejection off as the publisher's loss or a step on the way to success, which it is. We bleed for a while, and then we go on. The trick is to set things up so you can go on as quickly as possible.

Make a list of several potential markets, so if your piece is rejected, you can submit it to another publisher immediately. Keep three things in the mill, so you can look at the rejection you just received and remember you have other things out there. (With any luck, you won't get three returns on the same day.)

Keep pieces circulating even though you know you could rewrite them better. You can rewrite while the current version is out there. There is some possibility you will shoot yourself in the foot by submitting slightly inferior work to the best editor, but it is more likely you would otherwise keep the piece home while you wait to rewrite—and wait, and wait.

There is a time to ditch lousy work. You know, in your heart, when a piece is below par, when you're sending it out just to be sending something out. Don't waste the world's time with writing like this. Just go write something else.

Write a lot of something elses. One of the worst things you can do to yourself is make a career of one piece. Some people write two, three, four, five books before they achieve the smoothness an editor needs to see to make her want to publish. The same goes for short stories and articles.

To be successful, you must keep writing, learning, polishing your craft, creating new work, reading others' work, studying markets, rewriting, and submitting again and again and again.

# Two Paths to Publication—Summary

**Things You (Generally) Write First**

All stories, fiction and nonfiction
Creative nonfiction
Historical fiction
Reminiscence
Memoirs
Personal essays
Humor
Inspirational
Poetry
Opinion

**The Write-First Path
for Shorter Works**

Finish writing the entire piece
Edit carefully
Check publication guidelines
Prepare a cover letter if you
  are sending one
Prepare the manuscript
Submit the full manuscript
Keep track of submissions
Follow-up
Negotiate contract

**The Write-First Path
for Book-length Works**

Finish the book
Write your query letter
Have your full proposal ready to send:
  Cover letter
  Title page
  Contents page
  Synopsis
  Chapter outline
  Author biography
  First three chapters
    or first fifty pages
  Endorsements

**Things You (Generally) Sell First**

Articles
Profiles
Biographies
Business
Marketing
Self-help
How-to
Histories

**The Sell-First Path
for Shorter Works**

Research and write query:
  An engaging lead
  Supporting details
  Your credentials
  Contact information
Negotiate terms, rights, and payment
Complete the writing

**The Sell-First Path
for Book-length Works**

Query
Tailor proposal to agent or publisher
  Cover letter
  Title page
  Table of Contents
  Overview of book or a chapter
    outline
  Marketing information—a competitive
    analysis and ideas for promotion
  Author biography—your credentials
  Sample chapters or first fifty pages
  Endorsements—testimonials that
    might work on the back cover
Negotiate contract
Complete the writing

Figure 27. Two Paths to Publication—Summary

# 4. Be Creative

In old movies, all a writer has to do is write. An agent drives a hapless author to a cabin in the mountains and leaves him there with a case of canned beef stew and orders to "Finish the book." The author finds an abandoned rowboat, goes fishing, rescues the girl across the lake, brings her back to the cabin to dry off, the power (if there was any) goes out, and, well, you know. As the movie ends, the agent swoops in and rushes off with the finished manuscript, the girl heats the skillet, and the author splits kindling for the fire.

In real life, the agents, editors, and publishers who used to mentor writers are busy trying to keep their doors open. Writers have to manage their own careers, which means that until you reach the top few percent of wildly successful authors, you have to rent your own cabin. This is bad news and good news. Bad, because it puts more pressure on you. Good, because it keeps you in the world, intensely aware of the needs of readers, agents, editors, publishers, distributors, booksellers, and everyone who is a party to your success.

## Writers Find a Way

As I write this, more than thirty writers in my inner circle are having their books published, some by respected New York publishers, some by small, mid-sized, e-book, or self-publishers. If I cast the net a little wider, beyond the inner circle to people I just know, the number increases to over a hundred. To these book authors, add the writers who are seeing their articles, essays, poetry, and short stories appear in print or on respected websites and blogs. Despite the gloom and doom, there are plenty of opportunities and plenty of writers who are making it happen.

Wisconsin novelist Karen McQuestion had more than one agent representing her work, and at times publishers seemed interested, but none of the deals came together. After several rounds of spent expectations, she decided to take a chance on offering her novels for sale as e-books on Amazon's Kindle. Before long she had a following—readers were buying her books and asking for more. Then a Los Angeles film company optioned movie rights to her novel

*A Scattered Life.* Shortly after that, *A Scattered Life* was one of the first novels selected for hardcopy publication by AmazonEncore.

What's most important about Karen's story is that when one set of doors closed, she looked around for other opportunities and found a door she could open. If e-book publication had not worked for her, she'd have found another way, you can bet on that.

Doug Jacobson is a business owner whose first novel, *Night of Flames*, is a World War II story inspired by the wartime experiences of his Belgian relatives and his own Polish heritage. You've met him before in this book, when he came into my studio, asked what I thought of his book, and managed not to choke when I asked him if he was up for devoting two more years to it. Two years later, when he had a really nice draft, he skipped the agent step and went directly to McBooks Press, a well-regarded, mid-sized publisher specializing in historical fiction. The McBooks editors liked his query, asked to see the full manuscript, liked what they saw, and worked out a contract.

The next step was one that often unsettles first-time authors—when an editor makes suggestions to improve work you thought was finished. Doug didn't waste time balking. He took the suggestions, went back to the keyboard, and created an even deeper, better novel. *Night of Flames* was published in a well-edited, well-designed, hard-cover edition that would make any writer proud. As I write this, Doug and the McBooks editors are putting the finishing touches on his second novel, *The Dark and Silent.*

Stacey Kannenberg is a mom who saw the need for a small, accessible book to help parents get their kids ready for kindergarten. Although she had a good enough concept to interest well-known publishers, Stacey opted for self-publishing because she knew she could sell the book herself and didn't want to share the profits with an outside publisher.

She visited schools in her area, asking teachers and administrators, "If you could have this book to give to parents, and it didn't cost the school anything, how many copies would you like to have?" Then she took that information to local businesses and asked them if they would like to donate the books to the schools. With creative win-win marketing campaigns like this, Stacey sold more than 75,000 copies of *Let's Get Ready For Kindergarten!* She also published *Let's Get Ready For First Grade!* and started HerInsight, her own media company.

When Kirk Farber finished writing his first novel, *Postcards From a Dead Girl,* he queried a list of agents he hoped would represent him with traditional publishers. While working his way through the queries and rejections, this web-savvy writer spotted news of the first Amazon Penguin Breakthrough Novel contest and along with thousands of other hopeful writers from all over the world, submitted his novel for consideration. To his joy*, Postcards* was accepted, and the first chapter was posted online, where it received positive reviews. Kirk (and three other Redbird writers!) made it into the contest finals. This experience was not only exciting for Kirk, it was useful to his agent—yes, he did get one—who used his online success to interest publishers. *Postcards From a Dead Girl* was published by Harper Perennial.

I could go on for a long time with stories about people who not only write well but are creative in their quest for publication. The route from keyboard to reader is not as direct as it once was, but as one path to publication turns to quicksand, enterprising authors like Karen and Doug and Stacey and Kirk blaze new trails and find many ways to get through the woods to Grandmother's house.

## The Big Secret

When you have written "something good," when you've mastered the pen, look for opportunities to get published and figure out how to make it happen. Rather than waiting for someone to show you the way, use your creativity and lead your own parade. Put yourself on the agent/editor/publisher side of the desk to get a better understanding of what they need and how you can work with them. And once you start trying to get published, you keep at it.

That's it. That's the big secret.

# APPENDIXES

# Appendix A
## Sample Format for a Manuscript

Your name                                                    # Words
Address
City, State, Zip
Phone numbers
Email address

TITLE

by

YOUR NAME

This is a basic format for preparing manuscripts for reading or submission.

There are many variations of manuscript formats. This one will work for most types of prose–fiction or nonfiction. In all cases, read and follow the specific guidelines of the agent/editor/publisher. For additional tips on preparation, see *Formatting & Submitting Your Manuscript* and *Writer's Market*, both published by Writer's Digest Books.

Set margins at one inch, and align left (do not justify). Select a plain font such as Times Roman, 12 point. Single space your contact information at the top left of the first page. Type your word count at the top right. The title and your name are centered, in caps, one-third of the way down the page. The text begins four lines down from your name and is double spaced throughout. Indent paragraphs. Avoid colors and fancy graphics. Minimize use of italics, bolds, underlines, and exclamation marks.

Do not put a page number on the first page.

On subsequent pages, put your last name and the slug (a short form of your title) in the left header, and the page number in the right header.

If you are submitting a hard copy, print on one side of plain white paper. Use a paperclip, butterfly clamp, or book box to secure the pages. Enclose a self-addressed, stamped envelope (SASE) large enough to hold your manuscript, or note that this is a disposable copy and send a self-addressed, stamped post card to be used for notification. Be sure to write the name and address of the publisher in the return area of the envelope or card, and include sufficient postage. Keep a copy of your manuscript and a record of your submissions.

In all cases, check and follow the agent/editor/publisher guidelines about submissions. Some prefer print, most prefer electronic; some like attachments, some don't. You will find guidelines in the market guides. Be sure to check online to see if names or instructions have changed since the guide was printed.

At the end of your manuscript, type THE END at the left margin.

THE END

# Appendix B
## Sample Format for a Cover or Query Letter

Your Name
Address, City, State, Zip
Phone numbers, Email address
[Or Use Letterhead]

Agent/Editor/Publisher Name                                    Date
Title
Address
City, State, Zip

Dear (Name):

This is a format you can use for hard copy cover or query letters. Adjust the format as needed for electronic queries, which are accepted by most agents and publishers. Always follow the specific guidelines of the agent/editor/publisher. For added tips on preparation, see *Formatting & Submitting Your Manuscript* and *Writer's Market*, both published by Writer's Digest Books.

Cover letters are sent with manuscripts you are submitting for publication. They may include:
- a reminder of prior contact
- details such as the availability of photos
- appropriate author information

Queries are basically sales letters for nonfiction you would like to write, or for a novel you have already written. The query may include:
- a few paragraphs designed to stir interest in the work
- mention of relevant experience (the reason you are the right person to write this)
- information about expected (or finished) length, resources, testimonials

Keep cover and query letters to one page, single spaced, with two spaces between paragraphs. Use a standard 12 point font with no fancy text or graphics. Align left (do not justify). Include note of any enclosures at the end, below your signature.

Close with a polite thank you and mention that you look forward to hearing from them.

Sincerely,


Your Name
Enclosures: [list each enclosure below]

# REFERENCES

*AMA Manual of Style: A Guide for Authors and Editors.* 10th ed. Edited by Cheryl Iverson. New York: Oxford University Press, 2007. Also available at http://www.amamanualofstyle.com.

*The Associated Press Stylebook and Briefing on Media Law.* Edited by Darrell Christian, Sally Jacobsen, and David Minthorn. New York: Associated Press, 2010. Also available at http://www.apstylebook.com.

Baldwin, Shauna Singh. *The Tiger Claw.* Canada: Knopf, 2004.

Bergstrom, Elaine. *Nocturne.* New York: Penguin, 2003.

Cameron, Julia. *The Artist's Way: A Spiritual Path to Higher Creativity.* 10th ed. New York: Tarcher, 2002.

*The Chicago Manual of Style.* 16th ed. Chicago: University of Chicago Press, 2010. Also available at http://www.chicagomanualofstyle.org.

*Formatting & Submitting Your Manuscript,* 3rd ed. Edited by Chuck Sambuchino. Cincinnati, Ohio: Writer's Digest Books, 2009.

Fryxell, David. *How to Write Fast (While Writing Well).* Cincinnati, Ohio: Writer's Digest Books, 1992.

Hanratty, Thomas. *The Art & Science of Tracking Man and Beast.* Milwaukee, Wisconsin: Medicine Hawk Publishing, 1997.

Hansen, Eric. *Hiking Michigan's Upper Peninsula.* Guilford, Connecticut: Falcon Guide, 2005.

Lamott, Anne. *Bird by Bird: Some Instructions on Writing and Life.* New York: Pantheon, 1994.

*MLA Style Manual and Guide to Scholarly Publishing.* 3rd ed. New York: Modern Language Association of America, 2008.

*The New Writers Handbook: A Practical Anthology and Best Advice for Your Craft and Career.* Edited by Philip Martin. Minneapolis: Scarletta Press, 2007.

Pamuk, Orhan. *Other Colors: Essays and a Story.* Translated by Maureen Freely. New York: Knopf, 2007.

Poynter, Dan. *Self-Publishing Manual: How to Write, Print and Sell Your Own Book.* 16th ed. Santa Barbara: Para Publishing, 2007.

*Publication Manual of the American Psychological Association.* 6th ed. Washington, DC: American Psychological Association, 2009.

Roerden, Chris. *Don't Murder Your Mystery.* Rock Hill, South Carolina: Bella Rosa Books, 2006.

Roerden, Chris. *Don't Sabotage Your Submission.* Rock Hill, South Carolina: Bella Rosa Books, 2007.

Roorbach, Bill. *Writing Life Stories.* Cincinnati: Writer's Digest Books, 2000.

Strunk, William, Jr., and E.B. White. *The Elements of Style.* Illustrated by Maira Kalman. New York: Penguin Press, 2005.

*Wired Style: Principles of English Usage in the Digital Age.* Edited by Constance Hale. San Francisco: Hardwired, 1996.

*Writer's Market.* Edited by Robert Lee Brewer. Cincinnati, Ohio: Writer's Digest Books, 2011.

*The Yahoo! Style Guide: The Ultimate Sourcebook for Writing, Editing, and Creating Content for the Digital World.* Edited by Yahoo! Sunnydale, California: Yahoo!, 2010. Also published online at: http://www.styleguide.yahoo.com.

# ACKNOWLEDGMENTS

IN ONE OF MY FAVORITE IMAGININGS, Henry David Thoreau is sitting beside Walden Pond, penciling vast thoughts in his notebook. His mom arrives with her Saturday basket of cookies. She brushes dust from her dress, sighs, sits down to rest. She has walked the mile-and-a-half from town. Someone has to feed the boy, you know.

In one sense, writing seems solitary—a writer staring at a blank page. But if you step back and take a wider view, it's clear that we never really work alone. Without all the others in our lives, we would perish for lack of cookies and pencils and the Internet and people who ask, "Are you finished with that thing, yet?"

In my wider view, I see Uncle Warren, my champion since I slammed my three-wheeler into a car and bled all over him. He and my big brother Bob were among the first to say I should shut up and write.

Ten years ago, my friend Mary Jane Johnson sent a firm note: "Write a book!" I still have the note. Other friends cajoled and critiqued, and listened to me whine until I decided to turn the writing from work into fun and just get on with it. Big hugs to Mary Lou Bell, Roi Solberg, Shauna Singh Baldwin, Jean Scherwenka, Felicity Librie, Laurel Landis, Jean Harlan, Stephen Boehrer, Sister Lourdette Van Driel, Allyn Travis, Kim Suhr, and the writers in the Redbird writing groups.

Annie Chase took time off from her novel to help with the research and create writing samples for this book. She and Jeannée Sacken, Anne Bingham, Sara Rattan, Marjorie Pagel, Carol Lachapelle, and Linda Mrochinski all pitched in to critique the manuscript and keep me on track.

From idea to index, my husband Dave Blank has been beside me. We were married the same year I founded Redbird Studio and started teaching workshops. I can't count the number of boxes he carried or computer programs he installed. He drew the red bird, designed my website, and banged on the door of a closed pastry shop until the baker answered and packed up a bag of peanut butter cookies for me.

My nephews and nieces, especially Kris and Katie Lance, abandoned their parents from time to time to give their Aunt Judy a hand.

I always knew that I wanted the team of Susan Pittelman, Kate Hawley, and Carolyn Kott Washburne to edit and design the book. I think you'll be as impressed with their work as I am.

# ABOUT ME

HERE'S WHAT I LIKE ABOUT THIS PICTURE.

The Shut Up & Write! doll was painted by my friend Mary Lou Bell. It reminds me of times she and other friends stood in doorways saying, "This way to the Judy Bridges workshop."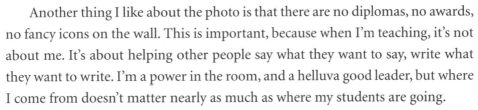

The tiny gorilla in the foreground is a mini version of my writing buddy Alfred, who lets me write nonsense when I want to.

The "book" in front of me is an early draft of this manuscript.

I'm smiling. This is normal for me. I still giggle, and I sometimes growl. But I am never, ever, passive. Not even when I try to be.

Another thing I like about the photo is that there are no diplomas, no awards, no fancy icons on the wall. This is important, because when I'm teaching, it's not about me. It's about helping other people say what they want to say, write what they want to write. I'm a power in the room, and a helluva good leader, but where I come from doesn't matter nearly as much as where my students are going.

If forced, I will admit to having a bachelor's in writing (fiction and nonfiction), a master's in adult education, and over a decade of professional writing experience. In 1993, I founded a writing center called Redbird Studio, where I taught more than six thousand kids and adults to write better than they did before they met me. Redbird was named "Best of" area writing centers by *Milwaukee Magazine*. I was honored as a "Woman Who Put Her Stamp on Milwaukee." I have a huge white binder filled with awards and articles about the studio.

That's all very nice, but when I look at this photo, I hear the voices of writers reading their work. I hear applause, and advice, and encouragement.

That's what I like about this picture.

# INDEX

*Note: Page references in italics indicate illustrations.*

# Order Form

## *Shut Up & Write!*

To order copies of *Shut Up & Write!*, please complete the form below.
(Feel free to duplicate this form.)

I would like to order _____ copies of *Shut Up & Write!* at $19.95 per copy.

**Total Cost of Books**                                                    $ _____

**Sales Tax** (Wisconsin Residents add 5.6%)                               $ _____

**Shipping & Handling**

$4.00 for first book; $2.00 for each additional book; Continental US       $ _____
$9.00 for first book: $5.00 for each additional book; Outside of US

**Total Amount Enclosed**                                                  $ _____

**Ordered by:** (please print)

Name _____

Address _____

City _____ State _____ Zip Code _____

Phone Number (    ) _____

Email (for confirmation) _____

**Ship to:** (if different from above)

Name _____

Address _____

City _____ State _____ Zip Code _____

*Checks should be made payable to:*
**Redbird Studio Press**
PO Box 70234
Milwaukee, WI  53207

For credit card and online purchases, go to the Redbird Studio website
www.redbirdstudio.com

*For quantity discounts, contact Redbird Studio at jb@redbirdstudio.com*